PRAISE FOR
WORKPLACE LEARNING

"This book puts its finger on something I have long held to be hugely important: the significant difference a learning culture contributes to performance at both an individual and organizational level. I would recommend that every learning leader reads this book and absorb its lessons. If you put in place the conditions for learning, then learning will begin to self-generate and solve challenges, and deal with disruptions before they escalate and do damage.

I always enjoy the way Nigel brings evidence to justify his claims and builds in really detailed case studies to back up and extend his overall argument. The result is a convincing case and clear authority. I believe that the time is ripe to reassess the idea of a learning organization and bring the concept of a learning culture back to the forefront of discussion.

I cannot recommend this book highly enough. It is an easy, yet profound, read and anyone interesting in strengthening the talent agenda and increasing the power and impact of learning in their organization should grab this book with both hands. I think that it will have a significant impact on large numbers of staff in L&D, HR, talent and organizational development. It deserves to do well."
Elliott Masie, Host and Curator of the Learning Conference, Corporate Learning Expert and Guru, Head of the Masie Center, Saratoga Springs, NY

"In a world that is becoming increasingly connected and complex, the only source of sustainable competitive advantage is an organization's ability to collectively learn, unlearn and relearn faster than the competition. Learning, therefore, needs to be woven into the cultural fabric of every organization to ensure that it can maintain a perpetual state of readiness to respond to the unexpected.

What's required today is a fundamental reframe on the nature and role of learning in organizations. One that seeks to create an organization culture that encourages generative learning where people collaborate to find answers to novel challenges that have not been encountered before.

As we evolve from a predictable find-it-out world to an unpredictable figure-it-out one, the need to cultivate a learning culture in organizations becomes increasingly acute.

Thankfully, in this masterful book, Nigel Paine has created a blueprint to do just that. Within these pages you will find a sound synthesis of the theory and research on what is required to build a learning culture and practical case studies that bring these ideas to life in a clear and compelling way. If you're learning strategy calls for building a more responsive, resilient and agile organization, ignore this book at your own peril.
Prof Tony O'Driscoll, Fuqua School of Business, Duke University

"I loved this book. It is right on the note. In a world that doesn't change, there is no need to learn. For creatures of all kinds learning serves to adapt us to our surroundings, so in a world of daily change we must become everyday learners. Everyday learners can only flourish in a culture that visibly values learning – one where the essentially playful, exploratory, and collaborative nature of learning is celebrated. A culture where people are engaged in learning. Read this book if you want to work out how to build such a culture of learning."
Nick Shackleton-Jones, PA Consulting

"In *Workplace Learning*, Nigel Paine makes the case that learning, happiness at work, and success in our turbulent environment are indelibly linked. More, this eminently practical book shows how learning on an individual level as well as enterprise-wide happens when the workforce is crystal clear about a meaningful purpose at work, and when people are empowered to share insight, take decisions, and act in the service of a bright future. And so, begins a virtuous circle: purpose drives the desire to learn, and learning brings the optimism, hope and courage so necessary in today's rapidly changing world. But, as Paine shows so clearly, learning is more than just a change in individual employees' mindset or knowledge. Learning that leads to fulfilment and success requires a learning *culture*.

Workplace Learning is a powerful book that makes a compelling and well-researched case for reviving—and modernizing—the concept of the learning organization. Building an organization that has learning as a habit, and sharing insight as a pre-requisite, is the easiest and most cost-effective means of sustaining innovation and unleashing creativity. This book provides the building blocks to achieve this and is an important addition to the talent agenda."
Annie McKee, author of *How to Be Happy at Work*

"Nigel Paine's excellent book provides a deep dive into issues of learning culture that should be the prime focus of every Chief Executive and every learning leader across the globe. In today's world, the speed at which organizations learn is their only guarantee for success. This well-researched book presents a compelling case for organizations to create a culture of continuous workplace learning. It outlines the major workforce strategies organizations need to survive and thrive.

I believe that it is an essential read for anyone who aspires to nurture a successful, sustainable and effective organizational learning culture. If we don't focus on learning from working as well as learning to work, we will fail to compete in an ever-changing world. I sincerely believe that those organizations that take his advice will thrive. Those that don't will likely die."
Charles Jennings, co-founder, 70:20:10 Institute

"In Workplace Learning, Nigel Paine has written an enjoyable and thought-provoking work on how organizations can thrive when they focus on building a learning culture.

This book is not only relevant but also powerful in making the case that culture is still one of the most important attributes when fostering continuous learning, which is so critical in the workplace now and in the future. I cannot recommend this book highly enough."
Kelly Palmer, Chief Learning Officer, Degreed

Workplace Learning

Workplace Learning

How to build a culture of continuous employee development

Nigel Paine

KoganPage

First published in Great Britain and the United States in 2019 by Kogan Page Limited

2nd Floor, 45 Gee Street	c/o Martin P Hill Consulting	4737/23 Ansari Road
London	122 W 27th Street	Daryaganj
EC1V 3RS	New York, NY 10001	New Delhi 110002
United Kingdom	USA	India

© Nigel Paine 2019

The right of Nigel Paine to be identified as the author of this work has been asserted by him in accordance with the Copyright, Designs and Patents Act 1988.

Index compiled by LNS Indexing.

ISBNs

Hardback 978 0 7494 9762 0
Paperback 978 0 7494 8222 4
Ebook   978 0 7494 8225 1

British Library Cataloguing-in-Publication Data

A CIP record for this book is available from the British Library.

Library of Congress Cataloging-in-Publication Data

Names: Paine, Nigel, 1952- author.
Title: Workplace learning : how to build a culture of continuous employee
    development / Nigel Paine.
Description: 1 Edition. | New York : Kogan Page Ltd, [2019] | Includes
    bibliographical references and index.
Identifiers: LCCN 2018050115 (print) | LCCN 2018050814 (ebook) | ISBN
    9780749482251 (ebook) | ISBN 9780749482244
Subjects: LCSH: Employees–Training of. | Organizational learning. |
    Occupational training.
Classification: LCC HF5549.5.T7 (ebook) | LCC HF5549.5.T7 P245 2019 (print) |
    DDC 658.3/124–dc23
LC record available at https://catalog.loc.gov/vwebv/search?searchCode=LCCN&searchArg=2018
050115&searchType=1&permalink=y

Typeset by Integra Software Services, Pondicherry
Print production managed by Jellyfish
Printed and bound in Great Britain by CPI Group (UK) Ltd, Croydon CR0 4YY

To David Puttnam
(Lord Puttnam of Queensgate)

He was the first person to really sow the seeds
of the ideas which have emerged here. A great believer
in the power of learning, and always committed to
helping people be their best. He remains a quietly
influential mentor and coach.

CONTENTS

PREFACE

This book was written out of a sense of frustration. I knew that the idea of a learning culture was really important and I could see that others agreed: lots of references, and lots of attention but not a lot of clarity. So, I went back to the literature and tracked the idea of the learning organization back to the 1980s and forward through to the present in order to point the way forward for the future.

I tried to answer three simple questions:

- Does such a thing as a learning culture exist? Is it the same as or different from a learning organization?
- If it does exist can you define it?
- If it exists and you can define it, is it important, can you build it, and does it make a difference?

Over the course of the research and the writing, I discovered much more. And I became increasingly bullish about the concept and its significance. Building a learning culture may be the one indisputable characteristic of organizations that will thrive in the 21st century. To build that organization requires thought about structures and processes; hierarchies and communities, as well as how you can help people build their lives and their careers in places that make them feel valued. This recognizes that an individual's growth and development ends up correlating with the growth and development of the organization as a whole. I realized early on that miserable people tend not to innovate! Toxic environments do not lead to growth or success either personally or organizationally. Purpose in work also leads to more fulfilled lives outside work.

There are countless stories that could not be included in this book, but I hope that the ones that I have included point to a strong and inexorable conclusion: that there is something important about developing a strong learning culture. It is a process to engage staff and a strong way to build organizational success.

I have tried to go beyond simply illustrating what a learning culture is, and offer practical first steps and a road map for moving forward. I believe in this so passionately that I want thousands of organizations to take their first steps towards building learning cultures that reflect their own unique shape and aspirations. The evidence is increasingly clear, that self-regulated learning, coupled with creativity and social skills, build flourishing workplaces and individual fulfilment (Chavez, 2018).

The future of human potential is linked to creating individuals who are adaptive, resilient and creative problem-solvers. And the role of leaders in organizations is to facilitate this process and engineer those outcomes, not for a few staff, but universally across the organization. That process is synonymous with building a learning culture.

Reference

Michael Chavez, Head of Duke CE at a conference in Atlanta, February 2018 quoting Dr Vivienne Ming, founder of the Socos think tank. https://www.socos.me

ACKNOWLEDGEMENTS

This book would not have been possible without significant contributions to my thinking, as well as huge encouragement from a large number of people. Some read early drafts of chapters, others helped shape my ideas; these were the brave ones who took on the unenviable task of helping these words make sense. I have a huge debt of gratitude to those who forced me to move from confusion to order. As always, I take full responsibility for any weaknesses or lapses of logic in this book, but fully extend my thanks to the numerous people who helped me make it as convincing as it could possibly be. There are many more on this list than I can individually name.

Those individuals and organizations that let me case study and interview were crucial for the book, as well as giving me a much clearer idea of what is possible in great, well-run organizations. I would like to thank Henry Stewart from the Happy Company, Ben Betts and Emma Sephton from HT2, and Kelly Palmer from Degreed for their time and commitment.

My great debt of thanks goes to Garry Ridge, the CEO of the WD-40 Company, where the conversations in the early stages really helped shape the ideas. And, of course, his company forms a key case study in the book. This connection to Garry was enabled by Sue Bradshaw of Blenheim Chalcot, who also read an early draft of the WD-40 case study.

Rod Willis gave me invaluable help and the broad context for the really important concept of collaboration, and the tools he developed really work and engender the right kind of conversation and understanding. I also had incredibly helpful conversations with Naomi Lockwood and Tony O'Driscoll. Both helped clarify my thinking about the relevance of a learning culture to a successful organization. Don Taylor's book underpins my chapter on technology and he let me hack at his solid model for implementing learning technologies. Julian Stodd helped refine my thinking on trust and much else. I also picked Martin Couzin's brain on numerous occasions to help cement ideas in this book. Nick Shackleton-Jones challenges my thinking every time we meet. Discussions with Gillian Pillans, and her insights into organizational agility helped formulate the complex relationship between learning and business agility.

I have an outstanding debt to Dr Peppe Auricchio from IESE Business School for his enthusiasm, support and ideas. His model informs Chapter 7, and that chapter is the better for it.

As always, I am amazed at the competence of Kogan Page's staff, along with their patience and support. They have been long-suffering over this project and my inability to decide, finally, when it was done and dusted. In particular, Amy Minshull, Megan Mondi and Lucy Carter gave me more time than I was due, but Stephen Dunnell my editor takes the gold prize for tolerance and support in equal helpings. I also want to thank Sophia Levine, who got this project off the ground at Kogan Page.

I have sat at the feet of Elliott Masie for well over a decade having my thinking challenged and assumptions dashed to pieces. He is everywhere in the book. Long may it continue.

There is a name I cannot omit – that is Erina Rayner, who put up with everything, including becoming my ad hoc graphic artist for a while! She is the one person I never dared challenge or contradict, and the fact the book now exists is a testament to her tenacity, support and persistence. I should also acknowledge the spark and stimulus provided by endless conversations with Dr Celine Mullins, Amy Burvall and Sharon Claffey Kaliouby. I relish these moments of clarity in a general fog of unknowing.

The staff at the University of Pennsylvania have been superb. Not one word of this book was written without imagining having to justify any assertions before my peers. Dr Annie McKee has been a boundless source of encouragement and support, and Penn CLO student Viju Menon's doctoral thesis will make a major contribution to the concept of learning culture when it is published in 2019.

Introduction

There is, it seems to us,
At best, only a limited value
In the knowledge derived from experience.
The knowledge imposes a pattern, and falsifies...

T S ELIOT, 'EAST COKER'

For the vast majority of people at work, many of the ideas in this book will appear beyond reach. Their experience has taught them to have low expectations at work, and that most organizations are relatively dysfunctional; most leadership is poor and self-serving, and learning takes place on a limited, need to know basis. If we look at the various reports that detail the number of employees engaged at work, the average percentage is around one-third. (See, for example, the Annual State of the American Workforce publication that is produced every year by the Gallup Organization and The State of The Sector produced by Gatehouse which covers Europe as well as the United States. Both reports are in their 10th year of publication and the needle has hardly shifted over those 10 years.) Work is tough, stressful and getting harder. Experience says this idea will never work or is an impossible dream.

This book explains and describes a different kind of reality that is diametrically opposite to most people's experience. That is why I am asking you to put the lessons from experience aside for a while, and to come with me on this journey. I think that TS Eliot made a profound point when he asserted that knowledge derived from experience can falsify. He wrote the words above in the middle of the second world war, where hope was in short supply, and his experience of that world determined his bleak viewpoint and pre-judged his expectation of outcomes. But he overcame that gloom and found hope and energy, and I want you too to try to put that scepticism aside as you come on this journey.

The simple truth that I am trying to establish is that, in the face of such dramatic changes in our social, political and technological environments, work must inevitably change as a result. There is a lag between the experience and the outcome, but there are organizations that point the way forward. The direction of travel is pretty much inevitable as part of the adjustment that has to take place for organizations to thrive in this contemporary environment.

I am convinced, and I hope that this book will convince you as well, that the only possible way organizations can navigate the complexities and the disruptions of the current environment is to create a workforce wanting to learn, who are agile and adaptable as individuals, together with structures that enable and enhance that. The new environment is collaborative as work works best when people come together to share ideas, knowledge and potential solutions. A learning culture creates that agile workforce and helps build learning organizations. This is fundamental and important.

The metaphor that I use throughout this book is that a learning culture is an organizational gyroscope. Just as a gyroscope in an aeroplane allows the pilot to maintain a level flight in spite of turbulence and thick cloud, and maintain a constant sense of where the horizon is regardless of what is happening to the plane, a learning culture keeps an organization steady, facing in the right direction, and allows it to overcome whatever disruption it faces from outside. Having a constant reference to the horizon is just as important for those driving an organization forward through turbulence, as it is for those flying an aeroplane in thick cloud and high winds.

A gyroscope is a demonstration of two separate forces. The first is inertia, and the second is precession. The gyroscope stays level regardless of how the external environment in which it operates alters direction. Precession, on the other hand, means that the gyroscope responds to forces acting on it by spinning in a conical movement rather than perpendicularly. Both of these characteristics have their equivalents directly in the establishment and implementation of a learning culture. A gyroscope mirrors the wider world and helps those in control of the microsphere sense the relationship to the macrosphere. The gyroscope is small but critical. Its role is identical to a learning culture's in an organization.

This book will strongly argue that a learning culture is not a nice to have, or an indication of organizational maturity, although both of those things are true. A learning culture will become the definitive pathway to organizational survival within the next 5 to 10 years. It is, therefore, worth addressing what a learning culture is, and how you might take steps to establish it in your own place of work. In difficult times, work will be more enjoyable, challenging and stimulating. That is a huge promise going forward.

The book will not apologize for taking you back to the beginnings of the discussions around organizational culture, and some of the seminal work that was presented in the 1980s and 1990s concerning learning organizations and learning culture. It is essential that we understand that context in order to be able to move forward in the present. It is pointless reinventing a wheel that was pretty solid when it first emerged. But it is also pointless taking ideas at face value that were built in a completely different world and imposing them without question in our radically different present. Therefore, the book attempts to move us forward and offer an agenda for action in the current climate and helps us make sense of what these concepts mean in their current reality.

I hope you find this book rigorous, accurate and above all useful. It is, like all my books, a deliberate and conscious pointer towards action rather than debate. I hope that the research that I have completed for you provides enough evidence to establish the credibility of the pathway I have sketched out, and therefore you can take action with some degree of confidence knowing that what I am illustrating actually works. The proof of that pudding is in the case studies embedded in the book, but the action that emerges comes from the analysis of what works and what does not.

The journey to a learning culture inside a learning organization is not straightforward and will take time. But there are benefits to the individual worker and the company from the very beginning as you begin to look clearly at the kind of workplace you have created, and see, perhaps for the first time, what it is like to work inside it. As you decide on your most important first steps you know that you will make the working environment better and more productive.

Setting the context

The *Financial Times* had a banner headline in February 2018 that concisely sums up, in only four words, the flavour of the age we live in. It encompasses any number of reflections on the current reality of life in the 21st century, from companies, governments and individuals expressed in countless articles. It proclaims: 'The age of instability.'

The accompanying article refers, explicitly, to the turmoil on the world's largest stock markets but it has a more generic application. As certainties crumble, and large and small companies wonder who or what will be competing with them, and how they can maintain competitive advantage when there are no guarantees and no safe bets, leadership has to evolve to rise to that challenge.

Companies have no idea whether their biggest threats will come from an unknown start-up on the other side of the world, or from their known mainstream challengers. In the words of the former US Secretary of Defence Donald Rumsfeld, given at a DoD news briefing in 2002 (http://archive.defense.gov/Transcripts/Transcript.aspx?TranscriptID=2636):

> There are known knowns; there are things we know we know. We also know there are known unknowns; that is to say we know there are some things we do not know. But there are also unknown unknowns - the ones we don't know we don't know.

Leaders have to face both ways at once and lead through unpredictability, instability and volatility. Just as old business models have failed, old leadership models are beginning to fail. But it is not just about leadership; the way we structure and organize the workplace has to evolve alongside these other changes.

This is summed up by the writer and former corporate human resources and talent leader, author and coach Dr Linda Sharkey, when she claimed recently, at a Duke Leadership Experience in Atlanta, Georgia (12 February 2018), that human development in organizations needed to be rethought from top to bottom, and that included leadership development. Organizational structures also had to be redesigned to facilitate co-creation and innovation, and they needed to be able to emerge and adapt. Finally, organizations needed to simplify processes to lessen top-down control and unleash productivity.

The three watchwords of this ambiguous future begin with optimism. If leaders believe that they can get to a better place, so will everyone who works there. *Optimism* leads to self-belief and confidence. Even if you do not know the answer, you can believe that you will be able to work it out. However, to 'work it out' requires the commitment and intelligence of everyone, not just a few people with senior executive roles. Therefore, the second watch word is *empowerment*. If you are scared to take a risk and feel someone is always over your shoulder ready to pounce, you will always play safe and never try anything different, and your organization will stumble.

Finally, we move into an era where *collaboration* is critical but never a given. This is our third key word. That is because we collaborate when we trust our colleagues, and we believe in the integrity of the organization. This implies that we have respect for their ideas and are prepared to challenge our own assumptions. And with collaboration and measured risk taking comes experimentation. The best and the most successful organizations will be the ones that constantly try new things, knowing that some will fail. Failure, when flipped on its head, is an intense learning experience. That is why in WD-40 Company asks of colleagues, 'What did you learn today?' and learning from failed experimentation is highly valued and widely shared.

The need to rethink work and learning is at the heart of this, but a different kind of corporate learning; one that is all pervasive and self-generating. A learning culture does not simply imply a lot of courses, high investment in formal learning, or even a Corporate University, but widespread curiosity, and radical questioning of what we do and how we do it. If you couple this with a fanatical desire to share and collaborate, and then experiment and articulate, you generate ideas and new knowledge that emerge from both inside and outside. So there is a constant process of building from outside in, and inside out. Top-down leadership does not begin to address any of these challenges and more often works against this process rather than supporting it. And, in the same way, current structures and focus do not enable organizations to react fast enough, or engage sufficient people with the necessary acute sense of urgency and commitment to move forward.

Where does culture fit in?

Part of the answer comes from an article for the blog Medium.Com written by the Director of Managed Services at the MCSA. He makes a simple point: if you want to transform your organization, you need to focus on its culture. He adds: 'Training and education is key to help explain to organisations how they can best navigate digital transformation' (Storrar, 2018).

Go one step further into self-managed learning, and you can move away from navigation and begin to deliver something far more important: acclimitization. And digital transformation is no different from any other transformational change, it is just more pervasive. Storrar is on the right track, but he does not go far enough; learning is, perhaps, the only way that people can not just navigate, but adapt and thrive in a world of rapid change. This is not just something that affects what they do at work, it impacts their whole life experience. And if that process of learning is not just a solitary experience, but is shared across an organization, the process becomes that much easier to manage and extend. As Storrar says, culture is the key! And in an organization that has a strong culture of learning, where learning is valued and learning together is encouraged and facilitated, transformation is not a trauma but a process that emerges out of learning.

These conclusions do not emerge from a hunch, or guesswork, and are not hope over experience, but a conclusion based on systematic research and the collective wisdom of thinkers and practitioners. And we should be bullish about it because a simple conclusion emerges: if we want to equip people to cope with the future, then their willingness and propensity to learn and share that learning is at the heart of that process.

A strong learning culture is a fundamental component for dealing with complexity and uncertainty. It can enable people to find pathways through and manage the new concepts and ideas that help them work out how to thrive in a world where the answers are not obvious. No other process substitutes for learning or replaces the need to focus on people and equip them with the skills and confidence to take charge and to work it out for themselves.

There is no real escape from the conclusion that lifelong learning and dialogue are essential ingredients for business success for the first time since the industrial revolution. The fundamental aim of this book is to make the strongest case possible, to prove the efficacy of, and the need for, an enduring culture of learning inside every organization. In addition, this books aims to help and support those who want to take the critical first steps in building a learning culture in their workplace, and in so doing, create a sustainable model for change and transformation now and into the future.

Reference

Storrar, T (2018) *Digital Transformation – Why Culture is Key*, Medium.com pub, 30 January 2018

PART ONE
Exploring the concepts of learning culture and learning organization

Where did a learning culture come from?

Context

Those who work in the area of people and organizational development need to be clear about what a learning culture is. The term is being increasingly bandied about with looser and looser meaning attached. It is clearly a good thing – but we do not know how good or why!

The purpose of this chapter is to take the concept of organizational culture back to its roots and then situate the concept of a learning culture within that frame. What is clear is that these two terms are not the same, but the conditions for the latter depend to a huge extent on the nature of the former. Poor organizational cultures with a lack of trust and disengaged staff, with a climate of fear at their heart, will never build the conditions for a learning culture, or sustain one.

That is not to say that a learning culture has nothing to do with learning. In the case study later in the chapter, I trace how a learning leader can work with the organization to build that culture, and there is much in the remit of a learning team that can make a huge difference in favour of or against a learning culture.

The trajectory of the chapter takes us through Josh Bersin and Towards Maturity's models for developing a learning culture and offers up Marcia Connor's learning culture self-audit to help the reader shape their ideas and assist them on the vital first steps of the learning culture journey. Microsoft is used as an example of an organization transforming rapidly and consciously, under the watchful and dynamic eye of their new CEO, into a highly complex learning organization, as the company builds a deep and organization-wide learning culture. A short case study is then offered to show the journey one organization took from a traditional attitude to learning to a serious and nascent learning culture.

All of the elements listed above provide some indication of the way to move forward if you are committed to redefining the culture of your organization and building a strong learning culture. No element has all the answers and there is no magic formula, but the combination of insights should help you along that journey.

The link between organizational culture and learning culture

What is organizational culture?

As soon as anyone speaks about organizational culture, one name leaps out from the extensive bibliography of the subject. That person really defined the field almost 40 years ago: the MIT Professor Edgar H Schein. His seminal book on the topic, *Organizational Culture and Leadership*, is now in its fifth edition, having first been published in the 1980s. Edgar Schein's son Peter co-authored the fifth edition (2016) and points out the trajectory of organizational culture across those 40 years. That concept has morphed from 'being something everyone at work had a vague sense was guiding behaviour' to being 'touted as a firm's greatest virtue, [and] being leveraged for strategic change' (Schein, 2016). What was once barely articulated is now eagerly debated and actively managed. What emerged with hardly any conscious manipulation is now shared, developed and cultivated. What was implicit is now increasingly, and deliberately, explicit.

In a celebrated book that builds on Schein's research and ideas, *Cultures and Organizations: Software of the mind* (Hofstede, Hofstede and Minkov, 2010), the authors point out that each person absorbs many layers of culture. It is not a single thing or a single experience. It has many layers. The first layer emanates from the country or countries an individual belongs to, and their region or ethnic group also has considerable impact on defining who someone is. Gender plays a part, as does the generation that the person belongs to. Their social class and occupation are also critical. The final level is 'the way employees have been socialized by their work organization' (Hofstede, Hofstede and Minkov, 2010). This comes a long way down the scale of influence and is the last significant cultural influence. It is, therefore, impossible to discuss learning culture without at least an acknowledgment of the role that all our cultural experiences play and how they inform and engage with organizational culture, in particular.

The software of the mind refers to the mental constructs and assumptions that we all build, in order to make sense of the world and our place within it. It is a unique attribute of human beings. And it is no less prevalent in an organization than in any other manifestation of culture. These mental models are built out of a number of elements. Schein lists 12 of them. They range from small, observable norms of behaviour, such as when colleagues greet each other, to formal rituals and celebrations which include rites of passage, and traditions established when projects finish or rituals surrounding outstanding endeavour or reward and promotion. It includes 'espoused values', which define explicitly the nature of the organization. Google's exhortation, 'don't be evil', is an example of one such value. They help define the rules by which the organization operates, and the climate both inside the workplace for its workforce as well as how the organization is experienced by customers and by outsiders (Schein, 2016: 56–58).

But what is organizational culture in the first place? Schein favours a dynamic definition of culture. He sees it as: 'The accumulated shared learning of that group as it solves its problems of external adaptation and internal integration; which has worked well enough to be considered valid and, therefore, to be taught to new members as the correct way to perceive, think, feel, and behave in relation to those problems' (Schein, 2016: 61).

The process therefore has 'accumulated learning' at its heart as 'beliefs, values, and behavioural norms' are absorbed and adopted to the point that they are unconscious in the organization and the individual (Schein, 2016: 61). At this point they become a way of being, rather than a way of knowing. But this process is never concluded. As circumstances change, the culture evolves and adapts almost seamlessly as new problems are solved, new people arrive or the external environment changes.

Schein has continued to explore organizational culture over a number of decades and his model has become – if anything – more complex over the years. But one factor is consistent throughout his research, and that is his belief in the primacy of the CEO. In an interview with Tim Kuppler, which is on Schein's Organizational Culture and Leadership Institute website (www.scheinocil.org), he claims that: 'if you are really dealing with a cultural variable, like the degree to which it is constructive, you really have to start with the CEO. You cannot change culture in the middle... the culture piece is owned by the CEO, whether he or she admits it or not.' This simple but striking point can be illustrated by looking at the huge changes in workplace culture in Microsoft since Satya Nadella took over the running of the company.

The change of CEO at Microsoft

Satya Nadella became the CEO of Microsoft in February 2014, replacing Steve Ballmer, who had been appointed by Bill Gates in the early days of the company and took over the CEO role from him in 2000. Ballmer had signalled his intention to retire in August 2013 and that six-month search for a replacement had led to much speculation about who would be named as his successor. The role was seen as slightly toxic as Microsoft was underperforming; however, many outstanding CEOs had been touted for the role including the former CEO of Ford, and CEO of Boeing Commercial Airplanes Alan Mulally, who is now on the Google board of directors. But when the name emerged, it was greeted with a degree of astonishment. Up until that moment, Nadella had been a well-respected senior executive in the company running the Cloud Services division. He was not a Ballmer insider, and was not well known to the outside world... and he had never run a company. So, the naming of Nadella sent shockwaves through the tech industry sector. The appointment was perceived as a signal that big changes were needed at the company and that a seismic shift for Microsoft was about to occur. Many saw this as putting the future of the company at risk.

Although Ballmer had grown revenues by 300 per cent and doubled profits during his tenure, Microsoft's share price had stalled. It was no longer the poster child of Wall Street. While still being a huge, profitable corporation, its growth was slowing down and it appeared to rely on, essentially, 'old' technologies for the majority of that revenue (Nazario, 2014; Curtis, 2013). In a world gravitating from the desktop PC to the smartphone, Microsoft was locked into the past, and its attempts to gain a foothold, initially with its own Windows phones and then its purchase of Nokia, were both seen as expensive failures. Indeed, when Ballmer had been shown the first iPhone in a TV interview in 2007, he treated it as an alien object, and was reluctant to even touch it. And finally, having given it a cursory glance, he declared that it would fail in the market as no one would want a phone that did not have a proper keyboard with real keys! That interview appeared, particularly in retrospect, to sum up Ballmer as someone who simply 'did not get it'. And Microsoft was seen by many as a failing giant. No one was very surprised when Ballmer stepped down, but the appointment of Nadella was a completely different story.

In stark contrast with Microsoft was the fate of its once fierce competitor Apple – the inventor of the touchscreen smartphone. Apple's revenues had rocketed after the 2007 iPhone launch, and that process of rapid adoption created a shift away from tethered computers to a 'super computer in your pocket'. The rapid shift to wireless and mobile computing became a defining moment both in terms of technology and a younger generation's dominant lifestyle. So successful was this process that, in 2017, over two-thirds of Apple's entire company revenue came from iPhone sales. And its computer operating system, MACos, a competitor to the ubiquitous Windows environment, kept ahead of Windows and was updated every year. But unlike Windows the new version had been given away as a free download to its customers for many years so the vast majority of customers were up to date, and this simplified processes. Microsoft had to manage multiple iterations of its operating system, some of which (notably Windows XP) were nearly 10 years old. This turnabout in Apple's fortunes transitioned it from a niche player into the largest company in the world by market capitalization, a status once occupied by Microsoft at the turn of the 21st century.

Fast Company published an extensive interview with Nadella by Harry McCracken, the technology editor for the journal (McCracken, 2017). It is a sympathetic portrait of a CEO who is in the process of transforming that company. During his brief tenure, Nadella has already added $250 billion to the value of the company. This is a remarkable achievement in its own right, particularly as most of that revenue has come from new products and services, but this is not the focus of the article on Nadella; it concentrates not on his business strategy, but on cultural change inside the company.

The article recounts how, before he had his first executive meeting, he asked his senior management team to read one book: Marshall Rosenberg's *Nonviolent Communication* (2015). It is a book about the power of empathy and indicates how an individual can develop sensitivity towards others. With chapter headings such as 'Communication that blocks compassion', 'Observing without evaluating', and 'Expressing appreciation in non-violent communication', it espouses a four-part communication model that involves: 'what I observe' and 'what you observe'; 'how I feel' and 'how you feel'; 'what I need or value' and 'what you need or value', and finally 'the concrete actions I would like taken' and 'the concrete actions you would like taken'. These are expressed in terms such as 'would you be willing to...?' (Rosenberg, 2015: 266), rather than handing out instructions. It would have been the clearest signal possible, to Nadella's top executives, that things were going to be different, and the new culture in Microsoft would be far less abrasive and much more empathetic. The interviewer sums this up as:

> Nadella's approach is gentler. He believes human beings are wired to
> have empathy, and that's essential not only for creating harmony at work
> but also for making products that will resonate. 'You have to be able to
> say, "Where is this person coming from?"' he says. '"What makes them
> tick? Why are they excited or frustrated by something that is happening,
> whether it's about computing or beyond computing?"' (McCracken, 2017)

In Nadella's time as CEO a whole raft of new products have appeared, both hardware and software, and the company has shifted its focus to the cloud and cloud-based services. Alongside the new approach inside the organization has been a new alignment outside. Nadella is as interested in how a Kenyan internet café is leveraging Microsoft products and services, as he is in domestic corporate use. He is as proud of a book-reading software application, developed by a team in the Microsoft Research Centre in Istanbul, as he is in Redmond-developed software. His vision is holistic, and he appears to care about making the world a better place. And this new focus seems to be paying off handsomely. It is also hard, talking to Microsoft staff, to find anyone who has a harsh word to say about Nadella. He is widely respected and, just as Schein indicated, the culture has changed from the top and is now resonating through the whole company. This makes very good business sense and has created a sense of purpose and mission for the company, once again.

Nadella is a serial learner. His office is full of books; he reads constantly and expects his staff to as well. And his interests range far more broadly than the technology sector to which he belongs. This is clear from his choice of Marshall Rosenberg's book for his senior staff. So, at the heart of Microsoft now, is engagement with the world, attempting to learn from others and stay in touch with changes in Africa as much as in Washington State, together with a strong remit to learn faster and to share. At the heart of the organization that Nadella is building is a fundamental learning culture, from top to bottom, that will enable the company to react far faster to changes in its external environment than it was able to in the past.

Organizational culture and learning culture

We need to be able to differentiate between organizational culture and learning culture. They are clearly related, but they are, equally clearly, not the same thing. In this respect, it is useful to begin by discussing the work of the celebrated University of Pennsylvania Professor of Anthropology Greg Urban. He muses in an article that he wrote in 2007 about the continuities and differences between car models as they evolve over time (Urban, Baskin and Kyung-Koh, 2007). His focus is the 2004 Jeep Grand Cherokee. Car manufacturers always tout a revised model as 'new', but invariably it has the look and feel of the manufacturer, as well as the previous evolutions of the brand in past model years. Urban notes this seeming contradiction, and then explains it in cultural terms by redefining the concept of a 'shared cultural model'. Ironically, when corporations are shown those evident 'cultural continuities' they are disappointed! They prefer the image that constant reinvention suggests: 'Even when continuity is patent... they tout newness and innovation, seemingly denying the powerful role of the past as a force shaping the present.'

This perception encouraged the author to reject the enduring concept of organizational culture developed and refined over the last 50 years. The 'shared culture model', similar to the definition given by Edgar Schein above, is replaced by a more complex and uneven idea of culture. Urban sees culture almost as a virus. It is contagious and passes from person to person but unevenly. Some get completely contaminated, while others are not touched at all. It can also leap from one community or geography to another very fast, and the patterns of contagion are varied and complex. He calls this 'a circulatory model' because the transmission of culture is uneven. Permeation is not consistent as people absorb myths in varying degrees, and as cultural elements are absorbed they are reshaped in the same way that stories are reshaped in the telling and their movement is complex, straying often beyond their defined grouping into new areas. In Urban's words: 'The myth told by b to c is not precisely the same as the myth told by a to b... This is also a premise of much of the research on globalization of culture' (Urban, Baskin and Kyung-Koh, 2007).

For Urban, we can surmise that a learning culture is a natural cross-check inside an organization; it maintains, but also holds to account, the overall organizational culture. It does this by reference to the outside world. A learning culture seeks meaning and reference from outside and ensures that knowledge and insight gained is rapidly transmitted around the organization. A strong learning culture is the antidote and the enabler of Urban's 'circulatory model'. It holds the culture to account, while also acting as the transmission medium for new ideas and new realities and the agent for change. So, a learning culture feeds off organizational culture, but also ensures its evolution and longevity. And in a fast-changing world, it may be the only way that alignment can be maintained inside an organization, and between an organization and the outside world.

That is the reason I developed the idea of an organizational gyroscope. It stands as a metaphor for the way that an organization stays aligned, both internally and with the external environment. Gyroscopes are stunning pieces of equipment that allow you to hold one side without the device falling over. It keeps everything steady and balanced and seems to defy gravity. Without gyroscopes planes could not fly.

A gyroscope, like a modern organization, is in the process of constant adjustment. And a learning culture stops an organization collapsing because, when turbulence occurs, it helps the organization regain its own equilibrium. That process of holding a culture to account avoids atrophy and ultimately, therefore, avoids oblivion. And as the world outside changes faster, the gyroscope becomes more and more necessary as a tool to maintain a balance, while adjusting to those external changes. It is, critically, about moving forward without too many shocks and without too much turbulence. It is, after all, always better to know which way is up!

Building learning cultures: a conversation with Naomi Lockwood

I spoke to Naomi Lockwood, a learning and OD specialist with huge experience of corporate L&D in a career spanning roles in an NHS Foundation Trust, a pharmaceutical company, and an examination and testing body.

Her first point was to emphasize that the key to developing a learning culture was to work hard to shift traditional and often transactional training and development functions, into transformational learning and development (performance enhancing) teams. It is often the case, in the former model, that what is on offer, as learning, is a catalogue of courses that can be selected and taken. Staff are often given the option of choosing around one or two a year from the catalogue, making the choice sometimes on what looks interesting, rather than what is useful in terms of their job skills. In this instance, learning teams are on the fringes of the organization, a long way from strategy development and the corporate centre, but nevertheless trying to do good work, without the traction or the connection necessary to make a real difference.

Naomi has a track record of putting learning centre stage, and she does this not by offering more of the same – a fatter catalogue – but by developing cultures of learning across the whole organization. This changes everything, fundamentally, in terms of the role of the learning team and requires a shift in perception from them, the corporate centre and the rest of the organization.

This transition for learning teams is about working in partnership with the organization, by helping to achieve its goals and aspirations, rather than operating as an independent group outside the dominant direction of travel of the organization as a whole. In other words, learning strategies have to be developed that not only support and enable organizations, and the people within them, to perform at their best and achieve their potential, but to extend that role into building cultures of learning. She believes that a learning culture is owned by everyone and built by everyone. It cannot be imposed.

In Naomi's experience, three critical elements are required to build a learning culture and they fit in to a convenient acronym: ART. A learning culture develops when the learning is in *Alignment*, has *Relevance* and is *Timely*.

Alignment

This is a baseline for learning strategy: whatever learning is offered, it has to be completely aligned and contribute to the achievement of the organizational strategy. The way that you ensure this is by really getting under the skin of the organization at multiple levels – by asking questions such as: what is the organization's fundamental purpose and what is it trying to achieve? What are the frameworks of expectation here (job descriptions, performance management frameworks, strategies, values frameworks, competency frameworks)? What do people need to know that will help them get things done? What is stopping them now? How is learning viewed by key stakeholders?

If learning professionals do not understand these expectations, it is unlikely that whatever they build will ultimately be fit for purpose. Naomi's approach, therefore, goes further than arguing for an 'on paper' alignment between the organizational strategy and that of the learning team. Her model calls for an alignment of language, alignment to organizational culture and individual aspirations, and to the key performance indicators (KPIs) of the business.

Alignment is the key to shifting learning from its position on the periphery, in terms of perception and impact, to one of a core contributor of value. And shifting the output of learning from individual choice to a corporate and strategic imperative makes it a key player that can reinforce and enable the strategic direction of the company.

Relevance

Relevance is also a fundamental component. Learning has to directly help people execute their role, and it should enhance their performance. It is verging on self-indulgence if this is not the focus. In addition, any learning organization has to take account of and build on how people learn in practice, both inside and out of work. This means understanding where they go to solve problems, gain knowledge and skills, and use this direction of travel to help build capability. This is the point where greater integration occurs between the formal learning programme, informal and social learning, together with learning on the job (in essence, the 70:20:10 model).

As people's access to information and technology changes, both at work and at home, the modes of learning provided by the workplace should also evolve. In an app-centric, mobile and Google-search dominated world, our learning is immediate, delivered at the moment of need and is sufficient for our purpose. It should be no less impactful when learning at work.

It is also important to figure out who is doing the learning and for what purpose. There are many instances in classroom-based or virtual classroom learning where a participant says, 'I am not sure why I am here, but I was sent here by my manager'. These are the people who often do not see or understand the relevance of the learning for them, and it is of questionable value for them. They are hardly present.

When people undertake self-directed learning – from Googling something to watching a YouTube video – it is usually perceived as relevant because the purpose is clear: it is to solve an immediate problem, answer a pressing question, or gain an alternative, expert viewpoint.

An L&D team needs to build on these insights. Organizations that wish to develop cultures of learning need to adapt to the needs and the current experience of their learners and this often means minimizing the times you send people away on training courses. The key role for an L&D team is to enhance relevant learning, not multiply the instances of irrelevant learning. The team can add most value by understanding and engaging with what the individual does outside the workplace. There is an apparently unstoppable trend towards self-directed learning and augmenting it in line with organizational strategy and individual development goals. Learning needs always exceed what it is possible for the organization to deliver, so the learners have to remain in the driving seat in order to work out their own priorities.

Timeliness

Timeliness is the third pillar and is a crucial element of the full process. It is possible to exploit the pace of technological development to prioritize 'just in time' learning. This is simply fulfilling expectations rather than doing anything radically new. L&D teams can add value to people and organizations by ensuring anything they curate, contextualize, develop or deliver happens at the right time for the right people. The focus should be on getting it to the right people at the right time, rather than imposing a fixed timetable of delivery or dishing out learning on a 'the more the better' principle.

One example of old and new thinking is how induction for new starters is handled. The focus should be on timely delivery of what is needed to ensure the individual gets up to speed as quickly as possible, thereby ensuring optimum performance in the shortest possible time. Booking someone on a face-to-face induction two months after they start work, because the programme needs a minimum number to be viable, and then delivering set content, regardless of need or concern, is largely ineffective and a waste of time and money. Induction should be timely, targeted and individualized in order to add real value and do what it is supposed to do, ie introduce staff to the organization that they have just joined and prepare them for a specific role within it. That is what the organization needs from induction. It is more useful than setting up a three-day face-to-face course regardless, and then running it once every three months, irrespective of how many people started work and when.

Using the ART model

How do you use the ART model? In other words, how do you work out what Aligned, Relevant and Timely means in your organization's terms? The key to this is to build strong links between the learning organization and the rest of the business and thoroughly engage. And the best way to do that, in multiple industries and different-sized organizations, is to take the time to engage at multiple levels, and then listen carefully to what you are being told.

She found that surveying every member of staff to understand what would make the most difference to them was hugely profitable. The focus was always on what would enhance people's performance and help them realize their potential – not asking them what training they would like, or worse, attempting to sell programmes that had been pre-agreed by the learning team into the organization. Instead of creating a long wish list to add to the training catalogue, it is imperative to try to understand where the blockers to performance lie and deal with them first.

She also spent time engaging senior leaders, including the board, through a process of inquiry and conversation, trying to understand their vision for learning and development and beginning to articulate that on their behalf. She used the frame of learning to understand and reflect back the organization to key influencers.

In large organizations, Naomi has used the World Café approach invented by Juanita Brown. This enabled groups ranging from 10 to over 500 participants to have coherent and focused discussions on specific topics. World Café is a defined process that encourages groups to build on each other's insights rather than work separately. The process has multiple benefits, including getting quickly to a shared vision, and creating an organizational buzz about the power and potential of organizational learning, while also generating lots of data. If the focus is on learning it can reveal what a learning culture needs to look like in the context of a specific organization. And that provides a simple agenda for action. Once agree, it is then possible to create a comprehensive plan for the development and the activity of the learning team.

This collection of data, together with trying to understand the evolving organizational context, is a continuing rather than a one-off process. In addition, it is important to identify people in the rest of the business who simply 'get it'. They are the trendsetters and the influencers, and they usually have an acute sense of what needs to be done. These are the ones who should be recruited as champions and spokespeople to sell the ideas and the benefits of learning to the rest of the organization and act as role models. This coalition can go a long way to ensuring that learning and the learning team remain aligned, relevant and timely.

In addition to this process of securing an agenda and building relevance into the L&D offering, and core to the underpinning philosophy discussed above, are three critical enablers of any successful learning culture. The first of these is to secure the backing and active support of leaders and managers. Secondly, the organization needs to develop reflective practitioners alongside the third enabler, which is an engaged and proactive L&D team.

On more than one occasion in this chapter, it has been acknowledged that leaders and managers are crucial to the development and future success of any learning culture. If they do not take it seriously or flagrantly disregard the behaviours, success going forward is almost impossible. As an example, quoted by Naomi, when you hear staff in organizations arguing that they do not have time for learning it often masks a conflict with their line manager. When you explore a little more deeply, it is the line manager who has no time for learning rather than his or her staff. In this instance, individuals feel they dare not engage in formal learning as it is a career-limiting activity. It is, after all, managers who dedicate resources and investment within their teams, and often decide on promotion or reward.

Where leaders and managers are on board, they often create a positive climate for the learning and development of their staff. This does not mean merely signing off training request forms via an LMS, but rather understanding what kind of learning will enhance performance, meet individual motivation and unleash potential. And the best leaders and managers approach this holistically and understand that all solutions should include both formal and informal learning as part of a balanced mix, and couple learning with other kinds of challenges to help individuals move forward in their career.

These managers and leaders are the ones who encourage and support continuing development throughout the organization, partly by offering sponsorship, and partly by what they say and what they do. The opposite is also true: their negative behaviour can wreck any initiatives. If they are not brought on board, and if they see little value in what L&D is offering, or its positive impact on the team's performance, their opposition is almost impossible to overcome.

The second enabler is the need to develop reflective practitioners. If any learning culture is to flourish, there is a real need to reflect on what has been learned. This is partly about quietly trying to work out how the new skills or insights might be used to overcome some of the current work challenges, but also to think about how learning can challenge current assumptions. At a time when organizations need to become more adaptable and agile to survive, building reflective practitioners should be core to this process. We also know that the brain needs quiet time to process and build strong connections as it tries to make sense of the world (Royal Society, 2011). And it is also clear that reflective practitioners should not just emerge from the senior leadership. Organizations need reflective practitioners spread throughout the business.

An essential element of any learning organization is an established belief that learning is important and should happen all over the place, all the time, and not be focused on courses. The concept of the reflective practitioner implies that any insights gathered, and learning nuggets collected, can be captured, discussed and disseminated and find their way quickly into work. The aim is to encourage better and better performance, essentially owned and driven by everyone in the organization. The CEO of the UK's Learning and Performance Institute, Edmund Monk (2017), described it simply as 'learning is everywhere'.

Creating an environment where people are true citizens of a learning culture means that for them, each interaction, conversation, meeting and exchange is seen as a learning opportunity. There is a role for L&D teams in supporting and disseminating this. For example, they can offer practical guidance on how to encourage reflective practice. Reflection time can be encouraged at the end of a meeting, before everyone leaves the room, maybe only for five minutes, to discuss and consider what is agreed has been learned. L&D can encourage staff to keep journals, video logs or simply write down insights on sticky notes before they are forgotten. Allocating time at the beginning or end of a day (or both) just to think about what you have learned, or what you need to accomplish, can be performance enhancing and developmental. These things are small nudges in themselves, but contribute hugely to developing and reinforcing that culture, as they evolve into corporate habits and become the way the organization does things and defines part of the organization's values.

The third aspect is the evolution of the learning team. In order to keep up with changing technology, increasing complexity, globalization and the nature of work itself, learning teams must change. Every element of what they do has to be reviewed and modified. Their focus shifts to concentrate on how the organization can be helped to perform better, not how many courses can be run in a given time span.

In Naomi's experience, she has often found that traditional L&D teams are made up of trainers delivering courses, often without any alignment to organizational strategy. Even more limiting are those teams consisting of (often very enthusiastic) L&D professionals who simply commission other (often external) L&D professionals and act only as form processors and administrators. They are at two stages removed from the direction of travel of their organization.

The growth of L&D as a profession, and the enabling of the role of L&D professionals should be predicated on their ability to facilitate organizational learning, and encourage, sustain and enhance cultures of learning. It is important to build both the capacity and the capability of internal teams wherever possible, so that they can get alongside their organizations to ensure that learning is aligned, relevant and timely. It is almost impossible to outsource that process.

The skills of the new L&D professional are different to those of traditional trainers, and include: facilitation skills, research skills, marketing skills, influencing skills, digital content development, curation skills and creative skills. However, that skill set should go further to include process skills, such as working in partnership or stakeholder management, together with coaching and performance optimization, as well as programme management, user design, user data analysis, and even selling or negotiation skills. Finally, all learning professionals now need a deep understanding of how to encourage, sustain and promote the power of learning through experience.

If, ultimately, L&D teams are there to optimize performance (individual, team and organization) they have to understand how to work with leaders and managers to help them improve the performance of their teams. Ultimately, the ability to work with leaders and managers to shift the needle will encourage lots of small conversations to take place all over the organization that focus on performance. The implication is that these discussions will occur at regular intervals and should replace large, unwieldy appraisal conversations that happen once a year. The generation of a learning culture has the L&D team at its heart but they do not own it. This is a fundamental element of the new L&D function.

Summary

By developing a culture that encourages asking questions, reflection on practice and asking for feedback, most employees are more prepared to openly admit what they do not know and ask for help. This in turn helps build trust and encourages widespread curiosity and rapid innovation. This process does not need much in the way of formal structure, or people with specific roles, to manage it. It emerges naturally out of the day-to-day interactions among staff, in their teams, and with their managers and leaders.

In the light of this, the role of the learning team becomes much more about the contextualization of learning and making resources available at the right time and for the right duration. These teams no longer post 'playlists' of courses but create personalized and focused learning. This shifts L&D from the periphery to the centre of the organization. It encourages staff to act differently and do their work more effectively. Therefore, the process enables the organization as a whole to respond to change and manage it better. In an increasingly volatile external environment this process becomes an essential element rather than a luxury.

Learning and innovation

Depending on the context, it is sometimes necessary to practice L&D by stealth. Learning must sometimes be aligned with the risky edge of innovation. It should be encouraging experimentation within a safe space and helping those staff who have traditionally focused on always getting it right, to find the right place and the right opportunity to take small risks and mount small experiments and accept getting some things wrong. The aim is not to jeopardize the core business but to enhance it in a systematic way – by creating patterns of inquiry, learning and reflection that occur around the core, with minimum disruption, until the core itself is changed.

The creation of a learning culture is, in practice, a fundamental shift that emerges from and also changes the overall culture of the organization. Building cultures of learning increases the switch towards recognizing the power of learning that is more social, informal, aligned, relevant and timely. It is embedded in the way people behave and helps shape how people react in that culture. In this way it becomes part of the fabric of the organization.

'Building a culture of learning' does develop agile staff who have a collaborative mindset and a willingness to share. These are the by-products of the process. Staff focus more on what needs to be done and admit what they do not know and seek help to get things right. This in turn helps build trust and encourages the widespread asking of questions. This does not need much in the way of formal structures, or people with specific roles to manage this process; it emerges naturally out of the day-to-day interactions of staff in their teams and with their managers and leaders. Learning, therefore, becomes unconscious behaviour for the vast majority of staff. Learning is increasingly informal, shared and supported throughout the organization. The end result is increasing resilience and agility in the face of change, as well as a more stable and committed staff base right across the world. In many ways, these are the elements that become the strongest indicators of learning culture in action.

Developing a learning culture using Marcia's Conner's inventory of a learning organization

Marcia Conner is a US-based writer, consultant and blogger. She focuses on organizational and social change and describes her work as 'ensuring organizational cultures don't suck, where people can work together and tap into how they learn so they can attain personal and professional success. I refer to this as "being human at work"' (www.marciaconner.com/about). She has written widely on collaborative work and learning, including a 2004 book on learning culture (Conner, 2004). In that book, as part of her work on learning cultures, she developed a simple inventory for a learning culture self-audit. It comprises a series of questions that indicate whether an organization is pro- or anti-learning culture and to what degree.

She lists 13 pro-learning culture statements and 13 oppositional (anti-learning culture) statements, which the individual is asked to rank on a 1 to 5 scale where 1 is no, and 5 is a firm yes (http://marciaconner.com/assess/learning-culture-audit). The instrument will do two things. Firstly, it creates a framework that defines the parameters of a learning culture. For example, a learning culture has an environment for extended conversations, reflection and shared learnings and where personal and organizational learning is considered important. Essentially a non-learning culture is the opposite. Conversation is about blaming and scapegoating; energy is attributed to profit and corporate success, and information is shared on a need-to-know basis only. The scores from both columns are tallied and they indicate the propensity for a pro-learning culture or an anti-learning culture, and the strength of that preference. The questionnaire will also allow an organization to track its progress over time by answering the questions again after, for example, a process has been instituted in the organization.

Conner also suggests that any contentious area or areas should be highlighted for further discussion and debate. So, the inventory is not just a static instrument but a development platform to encourage organizations to build a learning culture and establish a simple benchmark to judge progress. There is much to commend in its simplicity. But this is a complex area and it may not add up to a learning culture if all the boxes are ticked.

Marcia Conner's parameters

The model of learning culture that Conner implies in her series of questions essentially comprises four key critical elements. The first is about challenge and questions. A learning culture is embodied in a propensity to ask questions and tell positive stories inside the workplace; secondly, that culture allows for reflexion and experimentation. Thirdly, learning is not just valued but encouraged and supported; and, finally, a learning culture exists when managers debate and challenge each other and set themselves rigorous self-development targets. These four elements offer a useful counter-balance to Naomi Lockwood's ART model, where learning is aligned, relevant and timely. But we still do not have all the answers.

Looking wider: Kofman, Bersin and Towards Maturity

Three new perspectives will help pull together the strands of learning culture and enable us to come much closer to defining not only what a learning culture is but how it is possible to build and sustain that culture.

We can dramatically broaden our perspective by examining a seminal 1993 paper by Fred Kofman and Peter Senge, published by the American Management Association. The article is called 'Communities of Commitment: The heart of learning organizations'. It helps us think more deeply about the nature of a learning culture. Both Conner and Lockwood are programmatic in their definitions. Do these things and a learning culture will emerge. In the same, but more complicated way, Senge (1990) defined a learning organization in terms of five disciplines to follow, 10 learning disabilities to overcome and 11 rules to acknowledge in *The Fifth Discipline* (see Chapter 2).

Kofman (Kofman and Senge, 1993) shares a very different perspective and argues for a much more holistic view. It is from this broader perspective that a learning culture emerges. He believes that organizations are held captive by increasing fragmentation and competition that is deeply built into our culture and our companies. His starting point is the very nature of work. Only when work has been redesigned as a learning process, and a learning experience, so that, in the words of Harold Jarche, 'learning is work and work is learning', will the rudiments of a learning culture emerge (https://jarche.com). People at work, in his view, should always be exploring, experimenting and debating what they do, and there needs to be safe spaces to share the outcomes of those conversations, fuelled by what Kofman refers to as 'generative conversations': conversations that question fundamental assumptions about practice. It is a narrative that constantly creates new opportunities to learn and new opportunities to improve work process.

> Building learning organizations, we are discovering, requires basic shifts in how we think and interact. The changes go beyond individual corporate cultures, or even the culture of Western management; they penetrate the bedrock assumptions and habits of our culture as a whole. We are also discovering that moving forward is an exercise in personal commitment and community building. (Kofman and Senge, 1993)

We are a long way from a list of things to do; we even move outside the sphere and scope of business, and into the heart of Western culture! The problem with this perspective is where do we start? It would appear that learning culture emerges from a radical shift in organizational culture, which in turn emerges from a radical shift in societal beliefs. At what point can we break into that closed circle?

Bersin by Deloitte produced an important report in 2010, 'High-Impact Learning Culture', written by the principal analyst David Mallon (2010). It is based on interviews and a survey that reached out to 40,000 training, HR and business leaders. The conclusions are the outcome of detailed statistical analysis. The main conclusion, which is clearly demonstrated by the evidence presented, is that creating a strong culture of learning increases business performance. Finally, the report case studies a number of companies where this is evident.

The report outlines 40 practices of high-impact learning cultures and claims that organizations can intentionally strengthen their learning culture by implementing those practices that are identified. Furthermore, the change has to be driven by the leadership and the culture needs to be constantly reinforced. Of his 40 practices, 25 must be owned by line management, eight by top management and seven can be implemented by HR or L&D. This business focus is a constant throughout the report.

His fourth conclusion is that the nature of the business strategy will change the nature of the learning culture. In other words, there is no such thing as a specific and identifiable learning culture that holds good for all organizations. Finally, the report concludes that a strong learning culture improves business efficiency, which he encapsulates into 10 critical business practices, such as learning agility, innovation, customer responsiveness, etc.

Out of all this complexity, Bersin identifies six core traits that can be observed as manifestations of a high-impact learning culture. And all of these have been mentioned elsewhere in this book and emerge directly from the case studies. The report describes an environment that: builds trust; encourages reflection; demonstrates the value of learning; enables knowledge sharing; empowers employees and formalizes learning as a process. Employees need to have an ability to learn together with the motivation to learn and the ability to acquire new skills and, critically, apply those skills or that knowledge into improved business outcomes. It is a relatively simple model that has more business-centric thrust than others, but is less daunting than Senge or Kofman.

Bersin's report operates from a diametrically opposite stance to the identifiable characteristics of a learning culture approach. He starts with looking at successful business strategies and defines 40 practices that emerge out of a successful business strategy. These are mapped to the development of a learning culture. So, on the one hand, Bersin plays down the checklist as being too simplistic, while simultaneously arguing for a conscious development of a 'culture of work' using his own simple model that is, essentially, a combination of inputs leading to identified business outcomes. These inputs are the core components of a learning culture, such as trust and reflection (listed above), driven by leadership and management through their employees who are motivated and able to learn, share and apply their knowledge. It is a model that has much to commend it and it is underpinned by both qualitative research and a number of detailed case studies.

Figure 1.1 The 40 practices of a high-impact learning culture model

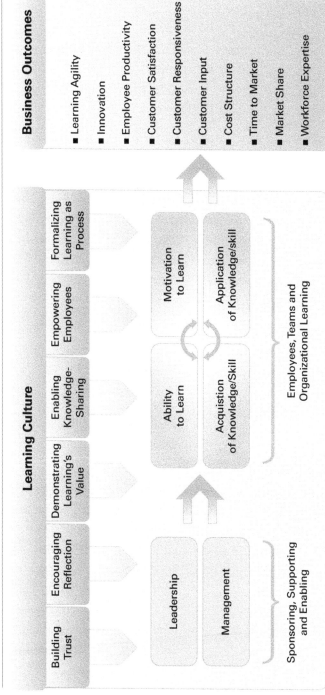

Learning Culture

| Building Trust | Encouraging Reflection | Demonstrating Learning's Value | Enabling Knowledge-Sharing | Empowering Employees | Formalizing Learning as Process |

Leadership

Management

Sponsoring, Supporting and Enabling

Ability to Learn

Acquistion of Knowledge/Skill

Motivation to Learn

Application of Knowledge/skill

Employees, Teams and Organizational Learning

Business Outcomes

- Learning Agility
- Innovation
- Employee Productivity
- Customer Satisfaction
- Customer Responsiveness
- Customer Input
- Cost Structure
- Time to Market
- Market Share
- Workforce Expertise

SOURCE Bersin & Associates 2010

Towards Maturity and Laura Overton interview

The final piece of the jigsaw lies in a 2017 report by Towards Maturity, 'Driving the New Learning Organisation', which was sponsored by the Chartered Institute for Personnel Development. In the Foreword, Peter Cheese, the CEO of CIPD notes:

> There are signs that the climate for the emergence of the genuine learning organisation has arrived. Principally, because learning itself has not just gone through an evolution, but a revolution. We have moved from an era when the course was the default learning approach, to one where skills and capabilities are developed through accessible and agile methods. Learning can now be delivered in the flow of work, not just in a classroom environment. Digital technologies facilitate learning anytime, anywhere and data enables learning to be targeted to need. (Daly and Overton, 2017: 4)

The research is based on the evidence from the annual State of Learning and Development survey that is now completed by close to 1,000 companies and has been gathering data since 2003. As a consequence, there are now longitudinal benchmarks available. Towards Maturity's conclusions are based on the input from over 5,500 senior people leaders from 55 countries (Daly and Overton, 2017: 15). This is a significant reservoir of data to draw from. From this research, Towards Maturity is able to isolate the 'top deck' performers who point the way for other companies in terms of their advanced practice and business performance. For Towards Maturity the clear distinction that emerges from the top deck organizations is their ability to remake themselves, and remain profitable and productive. A learning culture does appear to be an integral component of the business success demonstrated by these organizations.

I met with the CEO of Towards Maturity, Laura Overton, and she highlighted a number of critical factors that emerged from the report. It was clear from her research that a learning culture is not a facet of individual behaviour or organizational process, but a dynamic combination of both. There is no learning culture without identified behaviours leading to clear individual actions and a sense of responsibility towards your colleagues. But that attitude to learning emerges from the workplace values and processes. It is all about the way that the organization functions, and that is a product of the behaviour of teams and individuals as well as the processes and procedures established by the company. For her, 'It is much more about the outputs rather than abstract definitions. We always begin with business measures of success, and then deconstruct that success back to behaviours, values and attitudes.'

This is a similar process to the one used by Bersin and Associates. What Towards Maturity discovered was that there is one fundamental core attribute of a learning organization with a strong learning culture. And that is clarity of purpose. That purpose is clear to staff, customers and stakeholders. There are, then, five defining characteristics that bring that clarity of purpose to life and, essentially, translate it into action, process and business success.

The first is having what Towards Maturity calls 'an agile, digital infrastructure'. This is defined as: 'a virtual environment that enables a fluid exchange of knowledge, ideas and the adaptation of competence' (Daly and Overton, 2017: 8). Staff get instant help with immediate work-based challenges and are encouraged to work effectively together. In fact, it is second nature for them to collaborate and share both success and failure. This digital infrastructure requires a holistic people experience to make it work. In other words staff are offered new opportunities to learn and grow and are encouraged to innovate to improve the outputs of the company. This people experience requires a fully developed ecosystem that encourages growth and development across the whole extended enterprise. This will include 'board level accountability for organisational learning' and the promotion 'of a culture of self-reliance' (Daly and Overton, 2017: 8).

There are two other characteristics that Towards Maturity notes. The first is what they call 'intelligent decision making'. This is based on three behaviours: performance analytics to drive performance and the customer experience; clear business metrics that the company wants to improve through learning, and a watchful eye on emerging and best practice outside the organization.

The final characteristic is continual engagement, defined as: 'a dynamic community that continually builds on business relationships resulting in energy, resilience and growth' (Daly and Overton, 2017: 9). The model is shown in Figure 1.2 and illustrates the relationship between the core characteristic that binds everything else together – clarity of purpose – and the five others that emerge directly from it.

Essentially, Towards Maturity has identified an ambiance and a culture that has, at its core, engaged staff, encouraged them to push their own boundaries and, as a consequence, those of the organization as a whole. The only possible way to achieve this is by building learning into the heart of the employee experience, rather than as an adjunct to it. This is very much the philosophy of the WD-40 Company (see Chapter 5), where staff greet each other with a single question: 'What did you learn today?'

Figure 1.2   Continual engagement model

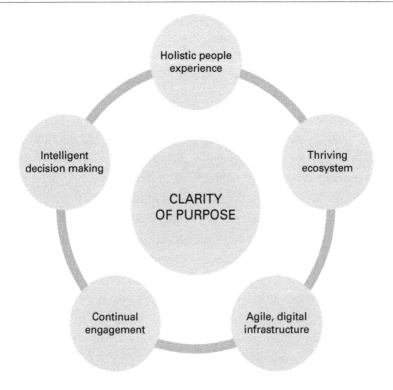

At the end of the report, suggestions are made to help both business leaders and learning leaders promote those six characteristics of a learning culture. However, one quote from the head of Talent and Organizational Development at the British Heart Foundation, Julie Jones, encapsulates the spirit and thrust of the report. She argues that 'Ensuring learning is within the DNA of the organisation and reinforcing the meaningful connection of learning to achieving organisational goals gives less of a "nice to do" and more of a "must do". We want to become a "we just do"' (Daly and Overton, 2017: 34).

The introduction to the report takes us back to Senge and his original vision, which is aligned to the new world of work. It claims that 'To effect real behavioural change in this new world of work, a future-focused business needs to bring learning and business leaders together to cultivate a "New Learning Organisation"' (Daly and Overton, 2017: 13).

I would argue that no learning organization – old or new – can exist without a clear and identifiable culture of learning. A learning culture describes the elements that make up a learning organization. You cannot fix the organization without defining and growing an appropriate culture of learning.

CASE STUDY Building a learning culture: the journey one organization took, and the contribution one learning leader made

Julia worked as the head of L&D for a large UK-based company. It is one of the largest providers of learning services in the world and employs over 2,500 staff, mostly in the UK but there are a small number running regional offices round the world.

When Julia joined the organization to lead a small learning team she found a very traditional operation. Essentially a portfolio of courses was served up in a catalogue of offers that staff selected and enrolled in. The target was each member of staff did two courses a year. This said nothing about needs being met or even what successful completion may have looked like. No attempt was made to measure impact beyond the normal 'did you find this course useful?'. In an organization dedicated to learning services, there was a remarkable indifference to their own developmental needs among the staff. The learning team were at the fringes of the organization doing good work, which was acknowledged to be useful, but was neither shaping nor driving the organization. The team were, essentially, order takers with no engagement inside the organization apart from ensuring delivery and uptake of courses.

Her agenda was to put learning centre stage, and she did this not by offering more of the same – a fatter catalogue – but by developing a culture of learning across the whole organization. Indeed, after six months of research, the strategy document for the organization as a whole about learning, and containing her aspirations for the role, was called 'Developing a culture of learning'.

The aim of the paper was to increase the value, perception and contribution of learning. The status quo was neither fit for purpose, nor delivering decent behavioural return on the investment the organization made. The big aim and challenge was alignment; shifting the learning organization from its position on the periphery, in terms of perception, to one of a core contributor of value. She was backed strongly by a head of People who wanted transformation of its impact across the organization in a way that got noticed by the leadership.

'Building a culture of learning' involved a considerable amount of careful research. Every member of staff was surveyed, with a 30 per cent-plus return rate; every member of the corporate board was interviewed, and a series of World Cafés were run around the organization. The aim was to look at the frameworks of expectation and outline what would dramatically increase the impact that learning made on the organization. This paper delivered one massive plus, which was to secure board support for the changes to be made. The aim was to increase the impact of learning in order to increase the organization's agility in the face of significant global challenges to its customer base and pre-eminent role.

The impact of the strategy was dramatic. The 'training' catalogue was replaced by six or seven key courses that were in demand, such as Prince 2 project management qualifications. This only formed 10 per cent of the total effort. Seventy per cent was spent on leadership and management development but much of this was outside the traditional face-to-face course format. The remaining 20 per cent was focused on developing core expertise within the organization. Individually oriented development, such as funding university qualifications, was deleted from the learning budget and pushed back to the various businesses to fund if they saw the need. At the same time, budgets for bespoke learning programmes were pushed back from the corporate centre to the various divisions of the company. This meant that specialist and technical development that was outside the learning organization's remit was separately funded.

The underpinning philosophy that led to this change was based on three key learnings. The first was that any learning organization had to take account of how people learned in practice: Google was a significant competitor. If Google could discover the answer faster and more efficiently than the official learning routes in the company, then that is where staff would inevitably turn for information and the learning organization could endorse this and shift focus.

Secondly, there was a real need for developing reflective practitioners; staff who were capable of observing and interpreting some of the weak signals coming from inside or outside the organization and taking decisions about how to respond. At this time when organizations need to be increasingly agile, reflective practitioners appeared to be core to the future success of the organization, and not just at the senior leadership level but spread throughout.

The third insight was to recognize the importance of leaders and managers to the future success of the company and dedicate resources and investment accordingly.

Induction was another area that had to be tackled; induction that was not fast and responsive enough to meet the needs of people coming into the organization. It had to be delivered at the point that they came into the organization; it had to inspire as well as inform or it would be mostly ineffective. The traditional model of waiting for sufficient numbers to arrive before running a course meant some had to wait over seven months for their induction.

The big insight was that if the leaders and managers were on board, they would create this positive climate for learning and would integrate reflective practice into their day-to-day work so that it became an integrated part of the culture. They would be the ones who would encourage and support continuing development throughout the organization, partly by offering sponsorship and partly by what they said and what they did. The opposite was also true: they could be the ones to wreck any initiatives if they were not brought on board and if no one had helped them see the value of what L&D was attempting.

In addition, those people in the organization who simply 'got it' were recruited as champions and spokespeople to sell the ideas and the benefits to the rest of the staff. Three words became almost the motto of the learning organization: learning had to be relevant, timely and targeted. The truth was that the learning organization, before these changes, delivered the opposite: generic programmes, delivered when it suited the organization rather than the learner, which had limited relevance to day-to-day work or the larger needs of the organization as a whole.

The broader philosophy was that learning should happen all the time, and not just on courses. The concept of the reflective practitioner meant that any insights gathered and learning nuggets collected could be captured, discussed and disseminated. The aim was to encourage better and better performance, essentially owned and driven by everyone in the company, and not just by a few people inside the learning organization.

As an example, it became common for space to be allocated at the end of a meeting, perhaps just 10 minutes, to discuss and reflect on what had been agreed has been learned. Staff were encouraged to keep journals or write down insights on sticky notes before they were forgotten. All of these actions were promoted, knowing that all leaders and managers offered encouragement and support.

In all of this change, the learning team, too, evolved. Digital content developers were brought in, and the trainers morphed into facilitators. A new role of performance optimizer was created, to work with leaders and managers to help them improve the performance of the teams they led. They shifted the needle so that lots of small conversations focusing on performance occurred, rather than large conversations at set times in the year. Then the learning team morphed into the talent team, as they absorbed both staff acquisition as well as induction.

The big goal was to increase, rapidly, the agility of the organization. Julia showed that building a learning culture does develop agile staff who have a collaborative mindset and a willingness to share. These staff focus more on what needs to be done and are prepared to admit what they do not know. This in turn helps build trust and encourages widespread curiosity and asking the right questions. It does not need much in the way of formal structures, or people with specific roles, to manage this process. It emerges naturally out of the day-to-day interactions of staff in their teams and with their managers and leaders.

In the light of this, the role of the learning team was more involved in the contextualization of learning and making resources available at the right time and for the right duration. They did not post playlists but personalized and targeted the learning. This shifted L&D from the periphery to the ideas centre of the organization. The learning team encouraged people to act; it focused on enabling them, trying always to emphasize how learning not only helped individuals, but helped the organization as a whole respond to change, and manage an increasingly volatile external environment.

This was L&D by stealth. The word training was banished, and trainers became facilitators. Learning operated at the risky edge of innovation, encouraging experimentation within a safe space and helping staff who had traditionally focused on always getting it right to find the right place and the right opportunity to take small risks and mount small experiments. The aim was not to jeopardize the core business but to enhance the core business in a systematic way.

The organization began to emphasize the contribution of each individual to delivering the overall vision. The mission switched from delivering learning services to changing people's lives by extending their life opportunities. And in doing that, the organization made a positive impact on economic development alongside individual achievement. Therefore, an administrator setting up, for example, local delivery facilities, felt that she was contributing to improving people's life chances. Everyone had a good story to tell and everyone could feel that they were making their own contribution.

There were symbols of the power of learning everywhere. The images that adorned the walls of their offices were testimonials from all over the world, from customers sharing life-changing opportunities. Each note told a story of hope and endeavour. They were a permanent reminder of what the company delivered. They were not so much notes, rather symbols telling the story of what the organization had achieved. Stories like these were collected and shared widely through the organization. Wherever possible, the organization got its customers to tell their own story rather than telling it on their behalf.

To sum up, the changes in the learning organization encouraged a fundamental shift in the culture of the company as a whole and helped make the staff more engaged in their work and equipped for the future. Learning became unconscious behaviour for the vast majority of staff. Learning was increasingly informal, shared and supported throughout the organization. The end result was increasing resilience and agility in the face of change, as well as a more stable and committed staff base right across the world. In many ways this is a learning culture in action.

What can you take from this chapter?

It is clearly quite complex to isolate the factors that lead to a sustainable learning culture that drives and improves business performance. But this process appears easier than trying to define and specify a learning organization. Senge tried and failed to do this. It is the elements of identifiable practice and behaviour within an organization that drive the culture and indicate progress. If you focus on the culture element, the organizational element sorts itself out. I have tried in Chapter 9 to pull both concepts together.

If you want to build a learning culture, there are 12 key messages to focus on:

1 The organizational culture will help or hinder a learning culture. Therefore, fix the elements that will prevent a learning culture taking root before doing anything else. These key culture elements inside the organization are: developing trust, offering constant feedback on performance, and allowing open and honest discussion of errors and mistakes without allocating blame. Acquiring these three habits, without exception, across the organization is a good place to start.

2 A learning culture manifests itself in many ways that are oblique to learning. The learning emerges from those processes.

3 Technology is critical but not the dominating factor. If there is no space to share ideas or debate issues across the entire business, it is impossible to build the component elements of a learning culture. Sharing and conversation are at the heart of learning both face to face and virtually. And insight and knowledge have to be stored so that they can be found easily. In addition, using technology to support learner choice and offer an overview of learning across the organization can be extremely catalytic.

4 Learning emerges from social interaction, informal discussion and working out loud. These have to be encouraged and supported.

5 A course mentality works against a learning culture. The learning organization needs to sustain other modes of learning. Learning cultures do not emerge from fatter course catalogues.

6 The learning team – in particular the learning leader – has a vital role as facilitator and enabler. The team does not own or control the learning culture, and should not wish to, but they should try to develop, sustain and maintain it.

7 A learning culture is driven by behaviours across the organization, and from its top to the bottom. It is not a manifestation of a small part of the workforce. That is why the buy-in at the top is critical.

8 There is no learning culture when there is no endorsement from the most senior executives, and no constant, active encouragement and support from middle managers.

9 Everyone should feel responsible for their own personal development and look for ways of enhancing their skills and experience.

10 A learning culture helps the business perform, and it drives business objectives.

11 A learning culture needs to be protected, it needs to evolve, and it should be kept under review constantly. When the alignment with business is broken, you no longer have a learning culture. A learning culture will keep the organization aligned internally, and aware of the external environment. At the same time, it will provide the tools and the confidence to react to that environment.

12 A learning culture is self-healing and reflects the organization back on to itself. It is, therefore, tuned into what makes an organization tick, and how the external environment is changing. It may just be the most critical component for survival in this volatile and complex age.

References

Conner, M (2004) *Creating a Learning Culture: Strategy, technology and practice*, Cambridge University Press, Cambridge

Curtis, S (2013) Microsoft: The ups and downs of the Ballmer era, *The Telegraph*, 23 August 2013, www.telegraph.co.uk/technology/microsoft/10262853/Microsoft-the-ups-and-downs-of-the-Ballmer-era.html

Daly, J and Overton, L (2017) Driving the new learning organisation, towards maturity: www.cipd.co.uk/Images/driving-the-new-learning-organisation_2017-how-to-unlock-the-potential-of-Land-d_tcm18-21557.pdf 2017

Hofstede, G, Hofstede, GJ and Minkov, M (2010) *Cultures and Organizations: Software of the mind*, 3rd Edition, McGraw Hill Education, New York

Kofman, F and Senge, P (1993) Communities of Commitment: The heart of learning organizations, in *Learning Organizations: Developing cultures for tomorrow's workplace*, ed Chawla and Renesch, pp 14–43, Productivity Press, Portland, Oregon (Also in *American Management Association*, 1993)

Mallon, D (2010) High-Impact Learning Culture 2010, Bersin and Associates Research Report

McCracken, H (2017) Satya Nadella rewrites Microsoft's code, *Fast Company*, 18 September

Monk, E (2017) Introductory talk at 'Learning Live' in London on 15 and 16 September 2017

Nazario, K (2014) The lowdown on Steve Ballmer's salary, net worth, education and career history, *IT Pro*, 25 July 2014, www.itpro.co.uk/ strategy/leadership/22745/steve-ballmer-biography-the-salary-and and-career-history-of-microsofts-former

Rosenberg, M (2015) *Nonviolent Communication*, 3rd Edition, Puddledancer Press, California

Royal Society (2011) Brainwaves No 2: Neuroscience: Implications for education and lifelong learning, *The Royal Society*, February 2011, Section 2.5, p 15

Schein, E (2016) *Organizational Culture and Leadership*, 5th edition, Wiley, New Jersey

Senge, P (1990) *The Fifth Discipline*, Doubleday, New York

Urban, G, Baskin, E and Kyung-Koh (2007) Corporations and the meta culture of newness, *Journal of the Finnish Anthropological Society*, 32 (1), Spring 2007

Senge and *The Fifth Discipline* 02

Introduction

In recent years there has been a remarkable increase in the number of organizations that refer proudly to their 'learning culture' or claim to be learning organizations. One look at *Fast Company* (www.fastcompany.com) or any business journal will prove that. These topics and concepts around the learning organization, however, emerged out of, and were vibrant and alive in, the 1980s and 1990s. They did not go away but remained dormant and need to be revived. Although these ideas seemed to disappear from view and the key texts went out of print, nothing that they talked about has become irrelevant. The scholarly journal *The Learning Organization* was set up in 1994 in the wake of the huge interest in these concepts and, now in its 25th volume, it is still published today. If we go back to that first issue, Martha G White wrote:

> Learning and creativity are inseparable components of any successful enterprise. So how do we go about being creative? How do we find a blueprint with which to build a learning culture – in our business organizations, our political and educational systems – in ourselves? Creativity, clearly, will not flourish in an environment which is not dedicated to change. Learning, therefore, is a critical issue. (White, 1994)

Every word of that article could have been published today and it would still resonate. There is much value, therefore, in trying not only to understand those re-emerging concepts, but also how and why they were created.

These ideas were, at least partly, created by two influential works by two authors. In the United Kingdom, Bob Garratt published *The*

Learning Organization in 1987, which linked the concept of a learning organization to the evolution of the workplace into something more sophisticated and fundamentally more democratic. Meanwhile, in the United States, Peter Senge, an esteemed MIT Professor, published *The Fifth Discipline* in 1990. This powerful and highly influential book, subtitled *The art and practice of the learning organization,* claims – quoting on the cover a *Fortune* magazine article of the same period – 'the most successful corporation of the 1990s will be something called a learning organization.' That quote would have been just as appropriate on the cover of Bob Garratt's book!

Context

It is impossible to discuss learning culture and learning organizations without reference to Peter Senge's *The Fifth Discipline*. It had a huge impact when it was published and became a talking point in terms of organizational development and contributed to the debate about how modern organizations can be built that focus on getting more from people, that engage their workforce, and are therefore more productive and innovative than their peers.

That book has lost its mass appeal but its logic and support for systems thinking is still relevant, even if Senge's claims for the efficacy of his rules, laws and approach have proved less than transformational in the decades since publication. It is, nevertheless, a great starting point for any understanding of learning cultures and learning organizations.

The book begins with Senge but moves beyond his approach and brings his ideas up to date. It slots Senge into the wider debate, which still continues, about whether you can identify something specific that can be called 'a learning organization', and what difference that makes to business success. It is also important to explore whether there are any specific indicators that could help others decide if they need a learning organization and if so, how to build one.

We should not see Senge's book as a unique contribution that emerged from nowhere but rather as one of a series of books that demanded better and more effective workplaces. It is no coincidence that these emerged at a time of unprecedented changes in workplace culture and efficiency. The book was written in an era (the late 1980s) where workplace democracy was being debated; where the impact of Japanese quality improvement methodology was challenging the dominance of Western economies and their manufacturing industries and demands for more holistic workplaces that tried to humanize work were rife.

The questions concerned the nature of work in an increasingly knowledge-based and service-led economy where automation could do more for less with higher quality. There was open debate about how it was possible to produce better quality products that cost no more than the shoddy products they replaced. For example, it is no coincidence that the ISO 9000 quality standard was first published in 1987. This was an attempt to lay down a universal quality standard, having incorporated other national standards such as the US Department of Defence procurement standard, and the British Standard, BS5750.

This was also a time when personal computing was taking hold in organizations and homes. It triggered the first wave of digital transformation, and new companies such as Microsoft (founded in 1975) had set its bar high with its mission statement of a computer in every home and on every desk. Apple, founded in 1976, had built the world's first graphic interface computer, the Apple Lisa, which was released in January 1983. Apple brought those ideas to the mass market with the launch of the Apple Macintosh personal computer in 1984. In addition, Sir Tim Berners-Lee had invented (and given away) the World Wide Web in 1989, which he saw as a means to exploit the existing internet and create linked pages of information that would allow connected machines to share information and data and hyperlink between pages.

This was a future bright with technological change and optimism, and a belief that it was possible to do things differently, and better. A new connected and digital world was a tantalizing prospect that was held out to us, but spreading the benefits widely was a different question. How could everyone get on board in such a way that the opportunities provided benefited everybody rather than just a few companies and a few individuals? The serious and vexing question was how to get organizations to transform themselves, and build their own bright future. It was into this febrile world that Senge's book was launched and it was an immediate success. The 1990 first edition went through many reprints in the year of its launch. In a world of technology, Senge returned our focus to the human dimension of work, and on things that could be done to make that world better on a more human scale and empower organizations to do things differently and faster, not as a one-off, but as a permanent step-change.

What is *The Fifth Discipline?*

Peter Senge's book *The Fifth Discipline* is undoubtedly a key text in thinking about the idea of building a learning culture or a learning organization. It is far better known than Garratt's book with a similar title, *The Learning Organization*, which is discussed in the next chapter. It achieved considerable global success. For example, my own well-worn 1992 UK edition was reprinted three times in that year. The first edition was published in 1990, and even without its appendices, is over three times the length of Garratt's shorter and punchier book (see Chapter 3).

Senge, an MIT Professor, made considerable waves with this book. It was one of the must-have business books of the 1990s and created the traction and interest in its subject matter that Garratt's book failed to do. The two authors operated independently although both acknowledge the strong influence of the Harvard academic, Chris Argyris, and his work on double-loop learning.

This concept forms a bridge between the two works. Argyris talked about learning as an important constituent of organizational health for most of his long career, but the ideas were first elaborated in a book published in 1982 called *Reasoning, Learning and Action: Individual and organizational*. Argyris saw the link between clear thinking, successful organizational learning and organizational development. In a complex and challenging environment, the need for people to think better and learn more effectively was, in Argyris's view, self-evident.

Most people, he claimed, were single-loop learners, focusing on quick solutions to problems without challenging or even understanding the underlying assumptions that had led to the problem in the first place. To make progress you had to challenge those assumptions and take new approaches, or the problems would keep coming back. Double-loop learning was the only way to treat the disease, rather than the symptoms of the disease. The advocates of action learning, such as the academic Mike Pedlar for instance, saw action learning as a means of developing double-loop learning skills, because the process of questioning used by an action learning set gently uncovers hidden assumptions and challenges simplistic approaches such as rushing too quickly to the solution, or developing strategies for avoiding the problem altogether (Pedlar, 2008). It makes the participants think again, or think more deeply, and in so doing, uncover fresh insights that lead to new actions.

Both books have intellectual and geographical boundaries, however. You could argue that both books refer to their own academic and geographical clusters: Senge's is around Boston, with MIT and Harvard at the epicentre, while Garratt has his Trans-Pennine group with Lancaster and Salford Universities being his focal points. The motivation to write the books is shared by the two authors, who have a similar understanding of the issues and desire a common outcome: to create modern organizations that are, to a certain extent, self-healing. These organizations can constantly adapt to their changing environment and build workforces of engaged and aware individuals who all work in the organization as well as on the organization to make it function better.

What are the five disciplines?

Senge's book is, fundamentally, a systems thinking approach to developing a learning organization. He saw systems thinking as a core skill for understanding how an organization worked. He, like Garratt, saw organizations as a series of complex and interrelated elements. Systems thinking is a framework for analysing and understanding what makes organizations tick. Arnold and Wade (2015: 675) define systems thinking as: 'a set of synergistic analytic skills used to improve the capability of identifying and understanding systems, predicting their behaviours, devising modifications to them in order to produce desired effects. The skills work together as a system.'

This is a formal analytic approach that allows users to look at the whole rather than the parts and see the relationships between various internal and external influences. But when you look at Senge's definition of a learning organization you would not think that was his underlying approach. His fundamental definition is expressed in highly emotional (quite spiritual) terms, almost as an aspiration to a higher state of being. Learning organizations are 'Organizations where people continually expand their capacity to create the results they truly desire, where new and expansive patterns of thinking are nurtured, where collective aspiration is set free, and where people are continually learning how to learn together' (Senge, 1990: 3).

This is hugely engaging but sets a very high bar for the book to leap over. Who does not want to achieve what they truly desire, and have their aspirations set free! Later, Senge refers to: 'real learning [which] gets to the heart of what it means to be human' (Senge, 2000: 14). The seeds of disbelief and challenge, as expressed by David Garvin in his *Harvard Business Review* article published in the heat of the hype around Senge's book (Garvin, 1993), are sown very early. But Senge's framing words are percipient, and would pass unremarked upon today: 'The organizations that will truly excel in the future will be the organizations that discover how to tap people's commitment and capacity to learn at all levels in an organization' (Senge, 2000: 4).

When Senge called his book *The Fifth Discipline* he chose his words carefully. His fifth discipline is, of course, systems thinking. For him it unites and gives shape and structure to the other four core disciplines: shared vision; mental models; team learning; and personal mastery. And he is talking about a discipline, not a model. In other words, a practice that requires hard work and will continue to evolve and develop as the organization gets better at doing what it does. He likens his five disciplines to the five separate technologies that went into the production of the first successful commercial aeroplane: the DC3. All those technologies were critical and interdependent, but the creation of the DC3 was not the end of the line in terms of aeroplane development. Far from it. It was, in fact, the beginning of a whole new industry that refined each of those technologies continuously. Over a period of time, each of the five technologies was improved, so that each new generation of aeroplane was a step-change better than the generation that went before.

Senge believed that his systems approach would transform organizations over time, and he was outlining, or even bearing witness to, the starting point of a revolution that was unstoppable. This was the big idea that would revolutionize the world of work: he was convinced that he was building the DC3 of the modern organization, if you like. Work would never be the same.

I am sure that there is unanimous agreement that the 787 Dreamliner, for example, as an aeroplane, is a cut above the DC3 in every dimension, but its five core technologies endure and are still critical to its success. This conclusion would be unanimous, whether arrived at by an aviation expert or a fare-paying passenger. On the other hand, not everyone could point to the advances in organizational culture, or celebrate progress in organizational design, in the nearly 30 years since Senge wrote his book! The analogy does not quite hold good.

To complicate matters, it is also true that some of the most toxic business environments, such as the energy company Enron, for example, claimed a focus on talent, learning and innovation, and were aided in the development of their business model by no less a company than McKinsey (C William Thomas, writing in *The Journal of Accountancy*, 2002, shows the strong links with McKinsey). And the fact that this book is necessary, long after we should have been building multiple generations of the learning organization, indicates that, even if we can agree what we mean by a learning organization, the pathway to achieving such a thing, and the benefits that accrue, are by no means clear and straightforward. We have to update our thinking beyond Garratt and Senge to get anywhere near the answer we are looking for.

Senge (2000: 68) defines systems thinking as 'a discipline for seeing wholes. It is a framework for seeing interrelationships rather than things.' And Senge, therefore, recognized that having only a single focus on any one of his four disciplines would deliver a distorted organization and fail to create any kind of transformational change.

In other words, focusing your effort on building teams without the vision to see the direction of travel would not deliver success. To build a strong vision, without the processes and commitment to sharing learning, would be, ultimately, futile. Having a focus on personal mastery without team learning would fracture the organization irreparably, and so on. The holistic view was critical, and systems thinking brought the other disciplines into relief and delivered the benefits across the whole organization.

Systems thinking was also a way of coping with the increasing complexity both inside organizations and in their environment, as it helps develop what Senge (2000: 69) calls 'the antidote to this sense of helplessness that we all feel as we enter "the age of interdependence"'. Systems thinking helps us discern the structures underlying complex situations, and therefore the solutions to managing and changing them. This means that the whole could be changed as well as its parts. It is about focusing on interrelationships and process, rather than simply on immediate cause and effect.

Senge puts a lot of emphasis on the need for learning in context. In the here and now of work, not in abstract or in academic isolation. All staff, he argues, perceive the gap between the vision of their employer and the current reality in which they work. That tension creates aspiration, and encourages effort and a sense of heading towards a goal, both as an individual or as part of a team. If everyone is committed to pulling the organization forward that gap is positive and aspirational. Senge (2000: 153) calls this gap 'creative tension'. And 'truly creative people use the gap between vision and current reality to generate energy for change'.

The fact that we aspire and do not completely deliver the vision is not a failure. Senge would call this an opportunity to learn and a means of establishing clear goals; something to take advantage of and build upon, in order to push forward towards the vision. And that creative tension gives employees the desire and capacity to remake their organization and develop themselves. So understanding the current reality does not reinforce the negative sense of failing to reach the vision; instead it lays out a baseline on which to build. And all of this stems from building a commitment right through the organization to personal mastery: the aspiration to get better. This sense of purpose and direction has to come from leaders, initially, and stems from their own commitment towards growth and understanding. Leaders, Senge (2000: 172) insists, 'can work relentlessly to foster a climate in which the principles of personal mastery are practised in daily life. This means building an organization where it is safe for people to create visions, where inquiry and commitment to the truth are the norm, and where challenging the status quo is expected.' Senge's view is aspirational and optimistic. There is so much here which resonates in contemporary business and continues to set a high bar for the best organizations.

Seven learning disabilities

Senge's process is not just built on the five disciplines. He also outlines his seven learning disabilities that have to be overcome before a learning organization can emerge. And if that was not enough, he frames both in his 11 laws, which define appropriate overarching behaviours for organizations on their learning journeys. In many ways simply stating the five disciplines and the seven disabilities and the 11 laws exposes Senge's weakness. Where do you start and how do you keep all 23 in mind? His subsequent book, *The Learning Organization Fieldbook* (Senge, 1995), was an attempt to simply the processes and be more practically helpful. But the roots of over-complexity are never entirely left behind.

Senge's learning disabilities define what an organization has to do in order to prepare for its journey to becoming a learning organization: they all have to be eliminated. And that, in itself, is no simple task or quick fix. They define profound organizational mindsets that are complex to overcome and eradicate.

The first learning disability is 'I am my position'. If you define yourself by your position, you are unlikely to challenge any aspect of it or see the bigger picture or aspire to much beyond it. This also encourages an attitude where no one wants to take overall responsibility for anything or any failure, because 'I did my job, someone else must have screwed up'.

The second learning disability is 'the enemy is out there'. This is the tendency always to look for someone to blame. In organizations it can be those people in marketing, all the overpromising from the salespeople, etc. And if we cannot blame anyone in the organization we can always blame the economy or unfair competition from outside! It is the fundamental by-product of non-systems thinking and of single-loop learning.

The third learning disability is the illusion of taking charge. This disability describes the illusion of useful activity caused by rushing to action before really understanding the problem. The first task in a learning organization is to understand how the problems arise in the first place, rather than making an instant analysis of the cause, and then acting accordingly.

The fourth disability is the fixation on events. Senge believes that organizations are far too concerned with events whatever they might be, eg sales figures, budget cuts, quarterly earnings, and so on. This means that organizations tend to avoid the bigger picture or the causes of the patterns that generate the events. Senge (1990: 22) believes that the primary threats 'come not from sudden events but from slow, gradual processes', and if thinking is dominated by short-term events and reactions to them, then the generative thinking that is discussed about above cannot be sustained. A reactive organization is always vulnerable, always busy fixing things and rarely creative. This kind of organization is so fixated by action that it is incapable of learning.

The fifth disability, Senge calls the parable of the boiled frog. Whether or not this has been scientifically proven is unclear, but the story goes: if you put a frog into boiling water it will leap out immediately. However, if you put the same frog into warm water and then gradually increase the temperature the frog will become increasingly sluggish to the point where it can no longer jump out. The frog is effectively boiled! The metaphor suggests that organizations do not see what is slowly happening to them and end up in crisis. Senge illustrates this by reference to the US automobile manufacturing industry, which was slowly eaten away by Japanese and later, European car imports. It did not see the threat because it crept up slowly year by year, and percentage point of sales lost by percentage point of sales lost. By the time the US automobile industry woke up, it had lost 40 per cent of its market share. This happened over a period of 15 years. To avoid the boiled frog syndrome, organizations have to have antennae that pick up those weak signals and react to them. In the frenetic response to crisis after crisis or event after event the signals go unnoticed and therefore they are not acted upon.

The sixth disability is the delusion of learning from experience. Senge talks about our 'learning horizon'. A learning horizon is 'a breadth of vision in time and space within which we assess our effectiveness' (Senge, 1990: 23). Beyond our learning horizon, it is impossible to learn from experience and much of the time decisions that we make have consequences way beyond that horizon. Systems thinking is the answer to those limitations and that implies challenging our immediate assumptions of cause and effect.

The final learning disability is the myth of the all-powerful management team. This is the team that resolves the conflicts and solves the problems of the organization and sets its direction. However, if they are beset by the other six learning disabilities, they have very little chance of being successful. They end up defending their own territory and playing political games with one another. They appear cohesive, but they are in fact fundamentally divided. This means that disagreements are played down, and blame is handed out in order to protect positions. Dealing with any complex issue reveals the fundamental weakness in those teams. That is when the members work against each other and contradictory decisions are taken. If you can never admit you do not know something, or that you made a mistake and that other views apart from your own are valid, then that group can never coalesce as a high-functioning team. Senge, using Argyris to support him, emphasizes the critical nature of double-loop learning. Only by using double-loop learning can teams face up to contradiction and complexity. Senge rightly cites the dysfunctional management team as a massive issue for any organization. If that team is actively refusing to share or learn, the whole organization is paralysed and obvious issues are allowed to fester, or be made worse, by ineffective decision making. It is a definitive truth for Senge that no organization can become a learning organization when it has a dysfunctional senior team exercising poor leadership.

The seven learning disabilities are blockages in the organizational culture that prevent clarity, insight and effective action. They are indivisible; all have to be overcome before real progress can be made.

Senge's 11 laws

Alongside the seven learning disabilities are Senge's 11 laws. These are what Senge calls truths about organizations. Everyone has to be aware of and take into account these truths as they make decisions. Understanding these laws forms the bedrock of action that can lead to the establishment of a learning organization. They are:

1 Today's problems come from yesterday's 'solutions'. Failing to work out what is really going wrong simply compounds the problem. Hence the importance of double-loop learning.

2 The harder you push, the harder the system pushes back. This is called in systems thinking 'compensation feedback' so that an intervention generates a reaction in the system that undermines the intervention. Senge gives the example of a product that is losing market share. You react by dropping the price and increasing the marketing spend. This brings back a little bit of market share but that soon drops away. In the meantime you have used resource on the old product that could have been used for new products. He decries the idea that you solve problems by working harder to overcome difficulties. The key is to understand what is the root cause of the problem and deal with that!

3 Behaviour grows better before it grows worse. This is about the delayed reaction to simply solving obvious problems rather than the underlying issues. Fire fighting makes us feel better but it actually does more damage.

4 The easy way out usually leads back in. This is about applying familiar and often naïve solutions to problems by sticking to what we know best, and not dealing with the fundamental issues. It does not solve any problems in the long term.

5 The cure can be worse than the disease. This reflects the consequences of not looking holistically at issues and tackling small

parts of the problem without realizing the underlying effects and the lack of a holistic approach.

6 Faster is slower. In complex systems, we need to understand the system as a whole before it is possible to react to one event or other. Reacting instantly ends up creating more problems than taking your time to work out what is really going wrong.

7 Cause and effect are not closely related in time and space. Complex systems separate cause and effect – if you do not look out for the root of the problem you will rarely understand it, therefore really be able to solve it. We have to let go of the idea that cause and effect are closely related. They are actually separated in time and space.

8 Small changes can produce big results but the areas of highest leverage are often the least obvious. Small, well-focused actions can 'sometimes produce significant, enduring moments, if they are in the right place' (Senge, 1990: 64). This is about leverage. That is spotting the place where the least effort can have the biggest impact.

9 You can have your cake and eat it too – but not at once. Senge draws attention to the US manufacturing dilemma: you can either have high quality or low cost but not both. This thinking hampered the modernization of production and the modification of work processes to eliminate faults and improve production. There was a fundamental flaw: believing it was possible to work on one or the other (cutting costs or improving quality), rather than working on both, and improving both, simultaneously.

10 Dividing the elephant in half does not produce two small elephants. This is all about systems integrity and the need to work holistically and understand the complex nature of interactions the organizations generate. It also links to Garratt's frog and bicycle analogy (see Chapter 3). Dissecting a frog and putting it back together rarely makes a more efficient frog.

11 There is no blame. 'Systems thinking shows that there is no outside factor. You and the cause of your problems are part of a single system' (Senge, 1990: 67).

All of these 11 laws point very much in the same direction. It is about being systematic, thinking deeply and holistically as the only way to fix organizations. Essentially it is about changing mindset and worldview. A learning frame is an important way of challenging assumptions and helping encourage rich conversations that help broader understanding.

The energy company Royal Dutch Shell was a pioneer of scenario planning and established the basic guidelines for building and deploying scenarios for working out future direction. They established an entire department focused on nothing else (Cornelius, Van de Putte and Romani, 2005). Part of the motive for this was to challenge people's deep assumptions about the world, and therefore shift any ingrained mental models that they might possess and open them up to challenge. This allowed new worldviews to form and gel. So, therefore, building and challenging mental models goes hand in hand with vision and personal mastery. This is one way organizations cope with change and the unexpected. This is how they get prepared to throw away preconceptions. It requires reflection in the middle of acting and being self-conscious about decisions and stances, essentially being open to new ideas or approaches and being willing to change your mind in the light of the prevailing discussion.

Conclusion

What can we learn from Senge? And is his contribution still relevant?

1 The concept of the learning organization is far from dead. It is a rich, complex seam for investigation and exploration. However, what is equally clear is that Senge and Garratt do not have all the answers. If they did, there would only be learning organizations out there as the message about the importance of learning organizations would have been noted, and the processes for moving forward would have been implemented and embedded.

2 Senge is too complex. It is almost impossible to know where to start with his five disciplines, seven disabilities and 11 laws. He offers rich insight, and his observations on where organizations go wrong are still valuable, but there is no natural cause and effect. Even if you embrace Senge's message, you do not get a learning organization even if you do get a better, more effective and thoughtful organization.

3 The unifying principle elaborated by Chris Argyris of double-loop learning has endured magnificently across time. It is as relevant for individuals as it is for organizations and is simple to grasp and powerful to apply. That must be at the heart of the learning organization. The fact that significant corporations such as Amazon understand this indicates its enduring nature.

4 Returning to the thinking of the 1980s, which includes the work of Edwards Deming and Argyris, reveals the common roots for the two books that are discussed in this and the next chapter. Deming and Argyris were on to something important and enduring, and both of those thinkers changed the way companies behaved. Modern-day manufacturing owes much to Deming's pioneer work on quality improvement. Managing complex systems and getting to the deep root of issues and challenges still owes much to Argyris. In some ways, their thinking endures with more resilience than the two books that were influenced by those thinkers.

5 Understanding how complex environments work is still profoundly relevant. There is a major case for reviving systems thinking as a relevant tool for today.

6 The complexity of learning and its relationship to organizational development and improvement goes some way beyond some of the thinking behind the offerings from L&D in modern organizations. There is much to be commended about the more inclusive and holistic vision for learning organizations.

7 The need to focus on productive learning for today and generative learning for tomorrow, which emerges from the CRF report (Pillans, 2017) is a very helpful way of shaping complex learning from organizations, and shapes some useful ideas going forward (see Chapter 3).

8 We know more now about the nature of learning organizations, and how companies function in general, but there are still opportunities to move forward. In particular, the ability to connect learning with problem solving and idea generation is still in its infancy. It also outlines the core skills required to lead modern organizations. The concept of a learning organization says something helpful about how to deal with uncertainty and complexity. These are core ideas and spill out from the concerns of L&D alone.

Key learning

The fundamental challenge represented by Senge's book is related to complexity. In many ways, he draws our attention to the need to go beyond the superficial and the rush to find a solution. He makes it clear that quick fixes do not work, or certainly do not deal adequately with underlying problems.

It seems ironic that this movement forward into an age of micro-learning, instant answers to performance questions and a general granularity, and simplification of the learning process may not be the complete answer. The message from Senge is not that this is wrong, but there is a time and a place for everything. As the external environment gets more complex, and organizations deal with increasingly violent swings, both economically and politically, in their environment, some of Senge's logic is sorely missed.

Essentially, Senge is asking that we have a toolset that is able to address complex problems and get to their root. His methodology is based around Chris Argyris' double-loop learning and of course the fifth discipline itself: systems thinking. In many ways, the ideas expressed here have come again into relevance and prominence. This book is designed – in part at least – to drive people back to some of the thinking around the period when Senge was researching and writing. The book endorses these ideas and shows that they do not go away and are profoundly relevant today.

If you are involved in learning and beginning to think deeply about how you might help your workforce, in particular your leadership, rise to the challenges of an external environment that has unprecedented volatility, these nine suggestions for moving forward will be useful:

1 Slow down. Not everything can be dealt with in one paragraph or 30-second video. Recognize where there are difficult issues and be prepared to give those more time.

2 Think about how you will address some of those complex issues. Senge's 11 laws can stimulate some profound discussion about the nature of organizations. The fact that he refers to them as 'laws' is a slight exaggeration; they are more ideas about how organizations

ought to work. The ideas can galvanize a new understanding of what drives your place of work and can help leaders see the world in a slightly different light. This will help them focus on where the current decision-making process is not delivering. Think of examples in your workplace that exemplify the problems that Senge is attempting to address.

3 Focus on understanding some of your acute problems. Do not rush to find a solution; try to build in some double-loop learning. In other words, look at the causes of the cause rather than just accepting the superficial conclusion and rushing to fix it. For example, people fail because systems fail people. Blaming individuals does not fix the underlying problem.

4 It is often valuable to use action learning as a means of building shared understandings and solving big challenges collectively while gaining new insights from your colleagues. It is also a very simple way of ensuring everybody's perspective is recognized and taken into account. Action learning is, essentially, getting peers together to talk about their most pressing issues, and helping them come to an understanding of what to do (the *action* in action learning) based on an exploration of the issue by their peers, rather than an instant solution (Paine, 2017).

5 Recognize that time has to be allocated to grapple with thorny problems. This means that a focus on operational improvement and managing the day to day has to be balanced by some focus on building the kind of organization that you will need for the future.

6 It is absolutely vital that there is buy-in at the top. The general agreement that time has to be allocated in order to understand what is really going on, and what the underlying challenges are, has to begin at the heart of the organization and not in its margins.

7 The essence of Senge's analysis of organizations is that they are complex and organic. To get this message over to key leaders is hard but essential.

8 Ultimately you can work with Senge's idea for a long time without actually making much difference. The way to manage this is to boil down the many different options into two insights or challenges that you want to take forward. It is far too complex to think about

11 laws, seven disabilities, and five disciplines at the same time and know where to start. Think about what is most important to you and your organization, and act accordingly.

9 Senge is the starting point, not the end point, of this book. Keep reading!

References

Argyris, C (1982) *Reasoning, Learning, and Action: Individual and organizational*, Jossey-Bass, San Francisco

Arnold, D R and Wade, J P (2015) A definition of systems thinking: a systems approach, *Procedia Computer Science*, 44, pp 669–678

Cornelius, P, Van de Putte, A and Romani, M (2005) Three decades of scenario planning in Shell, *California Management Review*, 48 (1), pp 92–109

Garvin (1993) Building a learning organization, *Harvard Business Review*, 71 (4), pp 78–91

Pedlar, M (2008) *Action Learning for Managers*, Gower publishing, London

Paine, N (2017) *Building Leadership Development Programmes that Work*, Kogan Page, London

Pillans, G (2017) *Learning: The foundation for agility and sustainable performance*, CRF, London

Senge, P (1990) *The Fifth Discipline*, Doubleday, New York

White, M (1994) Creativity and the learning culture, *The Learning Organization*, 1 (1), pp 4–5

William Thomas, C (2002) The rise and fall of Enron, *The Journal of Accountancy*, 1 April 2002

Bob Garratt and *The Learning Organization*   03

Context and introduction

This chapter is a companion piece to the second chapter. It begins to untangle the ideas and confusions around the term 'learning organization', having attempted the same task for the even more complex term of 'learning culture' in Chapter 2. Together these two chapters try to establish a solid base for this book.

The starting point for the discussion is Bob Garratt's 1987 book *The Learning Organization*, which appeared to capture and encapsulate, in a short diatribe, the debates about organizational renewal and organizational effectiveness into an argument about the need for a different kind of workplace that encouraged more participation, created a more engaged workforce and established greater openness and democracy. The idea draws, consciously or unconsciously, upon Peter Drucker's incredibly far-sighted 1950s' concept of the knowledge worker as the 'most valuable asset of a 21st-century institution' (Drucker, 1959) and the notion of post-modern society where all assumptions about linear progress and direction were fundamentally questioned.

The chapter traces these ideas through to more recent research and links the notion of a learning organization to an organization's ability to build generative learning skills in the workforce, ie skills that enable agility, creativity, problem solving and innovation. Bob Garratt does not reference the work of Peter Senge and neither does Senge refer to Garratt's *The Learning Organization*. Both books, however, emerge from the same intellectual and business climate and are worth close examination, one following the other.

The underlying principle in both books is simple: you grow the ability and productivity of the workforce by increasing its capacity to learn and, in parallel, you develop the habit of sharing knowledge right the way through an organization. This cross-Atlantic flourishing of ideas around the audacious concept of the learning organization came from seemingly independent sources, as neither Garratt nor Senge quote one another in their respective books (although Bob Garratt does acknowledge the impact of the Senge book at the end of the revised 2000 edition of *The Learning Organization* (Garratt, 2000: 121) and notes the similar aspirations).

Senge and Garratt have different approaches to developing learning organizations, but there is an overall lack of clarity about what they are, and this increased very quickly as the idea took on a life of its own but seemed to leave the models and theories in its powerful wake. There continues to be an enduring confusion concerning the nature and clarity of the concept of the learning organization. It was an easy badge to claim without the need to define precisely what was being claimed.

This confusion was highlighted as early as 1993 in a *Harvard Business Review* article by the Harvard Business School academic David A Garvin reflecting on Senge's book. Just three years after the publication of *The Fifth Discipline*, he highlighted the difference between the idea and the reality of the learning organization: 'Scholars are partly to blame. The discussions of learning organizations have often been reverential and utopian, filled with near mystical terminology. Paradise, they would have you believe, is just around the corner' (Garvin, 1993: 1).

It is one thing, says Garvin, for an organization to acquire or create new knowledge, but quite another to apply it to what they do. This allows Garvin to define a learning organization as: 'an organization skilled at creating, acquiring, and transferring knowledge, and at modifying its behaviour to reflect new knowledge and insights' (Garvin, 1993: 3).

This is very helpful, and a good enough working definition that sees ideas, insights and new knowledge as important building blocks that can deliver action and change but emphasizes that the building and sharing of knowledge by employees does not necessarily lead to a learning organization. It is only when that knowledge drives the organization forward and changes the way it operates that the term can be justified. The link between knowledge and organizational effectiveness is not a given; it is fractured, complex and by no means a guaranteed correlation. What were Garratt and Senge actually saying? It is useful to examine both books, mentioned above, in order to pinpoint what they meant by a learning organization and attempt to show where and how the confusion begins. This will help us redefine the learning organization and make the term live again in the 21st century.

Learning and the workplace

Bob Garratt's book on the learning organization is only 122 pages in length, but it had an influence way beyond its word count. He claims that learning is critical for successful organizations because it churns insight between the outside world (customers), and the organization; and it helps the company talk to itself (it connects the majority of the workforce with their senior executives): 'organizations can only become simultaneously effective and efficient if there is conscious and continuous learning between three distinct groups – leaders who direct the enterprise, staff who deliver the product or service, and the customers or consumers' (Garratt, 2000: ix).

In Garratt's view, this not only leads to increased coherence and business effectiveness, but also to inherently more democratic organizations. This is the thrust of the book: the sharing of insight and knowledge between customers, staff and leaders inevitably results in more dynamic and more democratic workplaces that define the successful workplaces for the future.

Learning at the workplace is both the right thing to encourage as it creates meaning and belonging, as well as being a fundamental component of organizational health. In this age of social media, the concept of working hard to increase information flows between customer and organization appears quite quaint, as does the belief that increasing the rate of learning increases accountability and decreases corruption. Learning, in spite of Garratt's strong assertions, has not become a universal panacea. If you look at corporate cultures since the book was published, when technologies related to the internet and personal computing have dramatically increased access to information and knowledge as well as dramatically accelerated the flows of both around organizations and between organizations and their customers, there are few who would claim that this has led to a dramatic increase in accountability, employee engagement or democracy as the norm. And when you look at the scandals of the 2000s that erupted around companies such as Enron, to take one dramatic example, the focus on innovation and new ideas did not build strong, enduring organizations but corrupt and time-limited ones.

Enron revered innovation and ideas and recruited large numbers of very smart MBA graduates, but it could never be described as a learning organization. On the contrary, it withheld knowledge, celebrated a tiny elite, and delivered gargantuan corruption and fraud based on a naïve assumption that smart people with access to massive resources could rethink any process, and bring dramatic new profits to any organization bold enough to give them a free rein. When the idea failed, the company adjusted the accounts to make it look like the dramatic growth promised was still on target.

The corruption at Enron arose as the company made an increasingly desperate attempt to cover up the fallacy of this argument and hide the debt that was generated by a whole series of colossal failed projects that may have been audacious and creative but were also massively unsuccessful. The waste of resources that ensued eventually emerged into the cold light of day and convinced the stock market that things were not as they appeared in the company's optimistic public statements. The company may have been brilliant and mould breaking in many ways, but the ruthless pursuit of deals, and the need to demonstrate success at any cost, could not overcome the turmoil of the unanticipated collapse of the energy market in the late 1990s. C William Thomas wrote a blistering analysis of Enron in *The Journal of Accountancy* in April 2002. His conclusion was that Enron demonstrated 'individual and collective greed born in an atmosphere of market euphoria and corporate arrogance' (William Thomas, 2002). Understanding markets, using very smart people and allowing them to innovate, did not lead to success but rather disaster and jail sentences. Learning appeared to generate arrogance, and a sense of infallibility rather than enduring strength. How can the concept of the learning organization help us understand what went wrong and why? It was not just greed, but a corrupt culture that led to Enron's demise.

Learning and the rise of the smart worker

Garratt wrote *The Learning Organization* in the mid-'80s. It was written, in some respect, in response to the beginning of the acceleration of social and economic change in the developing world. This led to increasing uncertainty, coupled with a sense that productivity in British industry was falling behind other countries such as Germany, Japan and the United States. This coincided with the idea of the 'smart' worker, and a philosophy that the workforce had to be more engaged in their work, and to feel responsible for the process of making better products or services, rather than merely following instructions, in other words doing what they were told to do without question.

In the 1980s, large delegations were being despatched to Japan to learn about their remarkable production processes that seemed to do the impossible: produce ever-higher quality goods at less and less cost. Behind this – to a greater or lesser extent – lay W Edwards Deming's first hugely influential book, *Out of the Crisis*, first published in 1982. In 2011, *Time Magazine* named it as one of the most influential management books of all time because it introduced the concept of total quality management (without calling it that) and a template for what are now standard techniques in consistent, quality manufacturing. Deming's success in transforming industry in Japan in the 1960s was finally brought to America and then Europe in the 1980s. The book strongly argued for radical change. That meant rethinking the fundamentals of the workplace and turning the organizational pyramid upside down. This meant focusing on the knowledge and skills of the entire workforce, not simply on the brilliance of the leadership.

Garratt, however, is careful to note his antecedents. The book's relevance was located in the here and now, but the genus of the learning organization was tracked back to the immediate post-war period in Great Britain when Reg Revans, Jacob Bronowski and Fritz Schumacher worked together in the intelligence unit of the National Coal Board (the coal industry had been nationalized by the post-war Labour government) under the leadership of Sir Geoffrey Vickers. This is where small groups of leaders were encouraged to work together to problem solve and share their challenges. In essence, this method of problem solving became what we now call action learning. This process is discussed in detail in Chapter 9 of my book, *Building Leadership Development Programmes* (Paine, 2017).

The Coal Board's commitment to rigorous analysis created a climate for a new kind of decision making, and opened up the debate about what work was, and how you could make it both more fulfilling and more efficient. This intense discussion about more active workforce participation in solving the difficult problems faced by companies was the essential building block for the nascent ideas around the concept of the learning organization. Revans, we should note, developed his concept of action learning at the same time as Deming was working in Japan, and building his ideas around quality circles. In essence, they are exactly the same thing. Both are based on informed small groups of colleagues sitting together and working, in intense bursts, to solve their own complex problems without recourse to external experts.

Many of these ideas also became deeply embedded in Jack Welch's General Electric (GE). He was the long-term CEO of GE, the US manufacturing company. In 2000, Welch wrote in the GE Annual Report: 'When the rate of change inside an institution becomes slower than the rate of change outside, the end is in sight' (GE Annual Report, 2000: 4). In that same Annual Report, GE described with pride its progress in using the Six Sigma model (which emerged directly from Deming's concept of continuous improvement), digitization and dealing successfully with globalization. However, the real plaudits for GE's progress were attributed to working differently with its staff and building GE into a learning company:

> The initiatives are playing a critical role in changing GE, but the most significant change in GE has been its transformation into a Learning Company. Our true 'core competency' today is not manufacturing or services, but the global recruiting and nurturing of the world's best

people and the cultivation in them of an insatiable desire to learn, to stretch and to do things better every day. By finding, challenging and rewarding these people, by freeing them from bureaucracy, by giving them all the resources they need – by simply getting out of their way – we have seen them make us better and better every year. (GE Annual Report, 2000: 2)

The GE vision of setting smart people free to innovate is dangerously close to the Enron model. But the fundamental underlying difference lies in the wildly different cultures of the two organizations, and GE's laser-like focus on getting products and related services to satisfied customers. The problems arise not from the process, but when you lose sight of that core mission.

The development of conscious and continuous learning

The focus of Garratt's book is about developing 'conscious and continuous learning' between employees, managers and customers as I have shown. Essentially, that continuous churn of insight between what he defined as the three levels of the organization kept a focus, on both increasing efficiency inside the organization to do things better for the customer, and being close to the changing marketplace outside the organization in order to do the right thing for the customer. All actions by the leaders inside the organization, therefore, were based on their knowledge of the external environment and their customers.

Garratt dissected learning into three large pieces. The first area he defined as 'policy learning', ie engaging with and understanding customers; the second area was 'strategic learning', where the executive set direction in the light of their policy learning, and the third area is 'operational learning', which executes the strategy and makes it tangible. In the book, he acknowledges Reg Revans as his mentor, and the owner of that three-level framework.

Essentially, Revans' and Garratt's three levels are actually linked cycles of insight: three circles that overlap and impact one other. Focusing on the policy cycle builds customer insight and allows good strategy to emerge based on an understanding of needs. This is then operationalized. Policy learning, then, is about purpose, vision and values: keeping the organization close to the customer, so that the best decisions are made about operational efficiencies, and strategic decisions in terms of direction. So, according to Garratt, the essential conditions for a learning organization are that those three levels of learning share insights and inform each other, while operating independently.

The six pre-conditions for a learning organization

In order to explain how this might work, Garratt defined six pre-conditions before you can create a learning organization. These are belief systems above all and similar in concept and scope to Senge's Laws (see Chapter 2). Largely, they reflect the need for organic change inside the organization, refracted by changes in the outside environment. The precept is that business is becoming more complex because the world in which business operates is becoming increasingly complex. It is almost a biological model of evolution. As the environment changes, the fittest will adapt to those changes and thrive, while the rest will fail. This biological metaphor continues into Garratt's first pre-condition, which is the need to accept that 'organizations are complex adaptive human systems, not mindless machines'.

Garratt is drawing upon a whole raft of thinking around complex systems and their ability to adapt to a changing environment and linking organizational behaviour to biological process such as 'co-evolution' (Ehrlich and Raven, 1964), which explains how ecosystems develop in a climate of mutual support as they evolve. Garratt in a later article used the analogy of the frog and the bicycle to illustrate this point. This was an analogy used by many writers, including Mant (1997). A frog and a bicycle can both be divided into their component parts. However, when you try to reassemble (or re-engineer) them, the bicycle actually works better; the frog on the other hand is destroyed. Garratt saw organizations as frogs rather than bicycles (Garratt, 2000), and was, therefore, fundamentally and ideologically opposed to the prevailing destruction and reconstruction model of organizational change: business process re-engineering (Garratt, 1987).

Essentially, he saw organizations as complex systems that cannot be fragmented and reassembled without losing their identity and culture. Business process re-engineering reached its peak of popularity in the 1980s and '90s as a way of increasing organizational efficiency and decreasing cost by reassembling organizations after taking them apart. The idea was that the reconstruction would make them more efficient than they had been previously. This concept of business process re-engineering was crystallized by Michael Hammer in a now famous *Harvard Business Review* article in 1990. Hammer's war cry was: 'Instead of embedding outdated processes in silicon and software, we should obliterate them and start over. We should "reengineer" our businesses' (Hammer, 1990: 104).

Hammer saw organizations as machines that could be 'serviced'. Garratt saw this whole process as futile, because what looked more efficient in theory actually destroyed the essence of the organization in practice.

Garratt's second pre-condition is that 'organizations are driven more by process than structure'. Garratt believed that changing the structure of an organization was necessary but not sufficient, because:

> Sufficiency comes only through combining structural change with human learning processes to develop sustainable organizational learning. These processes must turn data into usable information fast enough to allow the organization to become more responsive and sensitive to those rates of change, externally and internally, so be able to adapt nimbly to survive. (Garratt, 2000: 15)

In essence, organizations need to be hypersensitive to the changes in their external environment and have reliable processes in place for translating that information into action. These processes need to operate across the three levels of the organization: the process level, the strategic level and the operational level. In this way, each level optimizes the learning from that data, but is informed by the interpretation and understanding of the other two levels.

Garratt saw the strategic level as the critical operator that sits between the process and operational levels, ensuring that data gleaned from outside is allowed to inform policy and is operationalized correctly.

In other words, those three wheels turn independently, but they are linked into a complex structure by cross-organizational learning.

Garratt's third pre-condition is based on the need to understand 'the difference between first and second order change processes'. Essentially first order change is based around a simple decision to do less of some things and more of others. It is focused on closed questions such as, 'why did this happen?' Second order change is when you take more of a helicopter view and reframe the issue entirely. This allows more complex learning and a more profound understanding of what needs to change. First order change quickly fixes what is obviously wrong; second order change looks more deeply and explores more complex issues and the broader patterns and contextual framework rather than homing in on the event and fixing those circumstances without looking more widely for the root cause. It is an exact parallel concept to the Harvard academic Chris Argyris's concept of double-loop learning.

The fourth pre-condition is 'accepting the need to integrate the operational and policy/foresight learning cycles into a formal strategic organizational debate'. It is one of Garratt's key ideas that the learning organization has to 'tap continuously into the natural, daily learning of everyone who is a member of the organization' (Garratt, 2005: 25). This process animates the learning cycles at all three levels and creates, in Garratt's words, the 'corporate brain'. Learning, therefore, is based on continuous serious debate and discussion around internal as well as external issues that concern not a small elite in the organization, but the entire workforce. Everyone should have a view and everyone should make a contribution.

His fifth pre-condition is about 'accepting and using the inevitability of "events"'. Reference to events refers to the supposed words of the UK Prime Minister Harold Macmillan in the 1960s; when asked what knocks governments off course, he is said to have replied: 'events, my dear boy events!' (This quotation is now disputed. See, for example, the *Telegraph* Article of 2002: www.telegraph.co.uk/comment/personal-view/3577416/As-Macmillan-never-said-thats-enough-quotations.html.) It was less eloquently expressed by Donald Rumsfeld. When asked to comment on the looting of Bagdad he replied, 'Stuff happens'. (The moment was captured on television: www.youtube.com/watch?v=RY9l73Yo9Pw.)

In other words, Garratt is suggesting that disruption to the smooth operation of processes and plans is an inevitability rather than an exception. Events (random changes) should be factored in when you operate in an increasingly volatile and confusing environment. Our systems should be sensitive to those changes, rather than trying to ignore or obliterate them. Sensitive in the sense of attempting to predict those changes, and pick up the weak signals that presage them, but sensitive, too, in dealing with these disruptions as and when they arise.

Garratt's final precondition is around the professionalization of those he calls 'direction-givers'. In other words, ensuring everyone has the skills to lead. Garratt laments the lack of proper development given to those who are selected to run organizations, right up to director level. He is a powerful advocate of professional development, leadership skills and coaching support. He argues that the process of choosing those selected to lead has little to do with their leadership skills or competence. It is based on expertise developed elsewhere. That blockage reverberates throughout an organization and prevents listening and learning. He demands that those key people should be subject to regular review and appraisal that monitors performance, and opportunities should not only exist but be prioritized in order to improve competence. Leaders need to focus on getting better at what they do. These are ideas that are now embedded in most organizations around the world.

Garratt also was an early advocate of what we now call the 'triple bottom line' (Savitz, 2013). He expected that any director should see leadership as a multifaceted task. It was obvious that a director had to ensure the quality of the business performance, but there was a second obligation to balance that: improving the quality of working life. The third obligation was to balance high-quality products and services with high levels of social responsibility and sustainability. And, of course, those directors had to be aware of, and committed to, Garratt's six pre-conditions before they could begin the task of building that learning organization.

How do people excel at work?

The book then looks in detail at how the three-level learning cycles are established, and ultimately interlocked around a framework of awareness raising and development. He traces a cycle where people begin to recognize their own unconscious incompetence. This sets them on a journey (via conscious incompetence and conscious competence) towards unconscious competence (Garratt, 2000: 39). As this applies widely to all employees, it therefore builds resilience in the organization itself. This is a staged learning journey that requires a sequential development programme for all staff, but is driven by leaders. And this process continues right up to board level. Garratt believes that employee engagement should lead to open discussion and a problem-solving mindset, where staff help each other to succeed. Garratt contrasts this process with the non-learning organization. Here there is no flow of insight and the organization is 'Full of blockages and has an emotional climate that encourages hiding mistakes and blaming others until the organization goes into a vicious and energy-destroying cycle of recrimination' (Garratt, 2000: 43).

In this case the learning is all political: how to hide, shift the blame onto others and avoid responsibility. The reality of what is actually going on is covered up and obfuscated. Enron perfectly exemplified this behaviour in the last two years of its life (William Thomas, 2002). So, essentially, Garatt is talking about building positive energy in an organization that is channelled into making the place better and more successful, in contrast to organizations full of negative energy, where huge efforts are invested in subterfuge, cover up, blame and ultimate failure.

The second contrast that Garratt describes is around job growth and bringing in learning from the outside. He defines a four-box matrix with top two boxes considering development in 'own job' and being offered 'internal exchange projects' or stretch assignments. The bottom two look at bringing in information from outside. The 'own job' side involves technical exchanges of expertise, and the 'other job' side is around external exchanges of new knowledge and new ways of operating. These are classic development strategies, stretching

Figure 3.1   Growth and blending

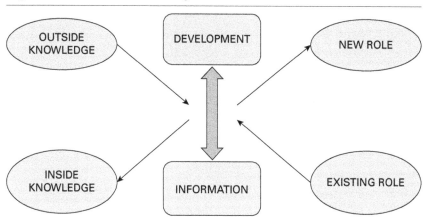

and challenging individuals to grow and improve in their work, while simultaneously encouraging employees to learn new skills and prepare for future roles and new challenges. It is breaking out of the 'my team' box to learning across the organization in communities of practice and encouraging linkages with the outside world to bring new thinking and insight into the organization. Again, Garratt is describing ideas that have since become commonplace.

This is explained in Figure 3.1, where existing role and stretch assignments blend with new knowledge and existing knowledge. Everyone works to develop themselves and the organization and bring insight into the organization to improve existing processes or develop new ones.

Is the idea of a learning organization dead?

Garratt made an important contribution to our thinking on how organizations can be more nimble and agile and get the best out of their staff. He did this in a way that takes account of the complex interrelationships between organizations and their marketplace as well as between the different levels of staff in the organization. His great strength is helping us see learning and insight as a continuous process.

Strategy is handed down, based on an understanding of the market, the customer and the existing processes. These insights are pushed upwards and inform that same strategy. His three circles, which represent three levels of organizational decision making and learning – the policy level, the strategic level and the operational level – turn independently of each other but overlap and therefore influence each other. Insight from the customer impacts the organizational strategy and its operating principles. Strategy is sense checked at the policy level before being operationalized, and so on. This is very close to Senge's fifth discipline (see Chapter 2), which is fundamentally a systems approach to organizational development. It too looks more deeply at cause and effect, and drilling down into the complex web of interrelationships that causes things to happen and problems to arise.

How to build a learning organization

Garratt's model is far simpler than Senge's and in many ways its simplicity is both its strength and its weakness. Garratt's concept of communication between the three levels of the organization and the resulting churning of insight is, fundamentally, his definition of a learning organization. But for that to happen, Garratt lists six pre-conditions. They are not functions of the organization, rather beliefs. If you cannot accept all six ideas you cannot build a learning organization, appears to be the conclusion. In summary, the pre-conditions are listed as:

1 Organizations are 'complex adaptive human systems not machines'.

2 Organizations are driven more by process than structure.

3 We need to understand the difference between first and second order change.

4 Policy and foresight learning should be part of the normal debate around strategy.

5 We must accept the inevitability of events.

6 Leadership should be professionalized.

They are part structural: there must be leadership development; part philosophical: you should accept the fact that organizations are complex adaptive systems; and part intellectual: you need to understand the difference between first and second order change. If you understand and operate in this way, the rest falls into place. History has shown that it is not that simple. However, what might have been seen as controversial and challenging at the time, appears less so now.

Recent research points to the complexity of business organizations and there is a growing view that biological models work better than mechanistic ones to explain how organizations work (for example: Reeves (2015) argues that biological models work better than models from physics to explain organizations) and business process re-engineering has been confined to the wastepaper basket. Yet we are as far away from building learning organizations now as we were 30 years ago.

The crux of the dilemma seems to rest with the complex relationship between the big organizational system issues, and the learning journey of the individual employee. They do not necessarily inform one another, as Garratt's model says they should. Becoming more competent as an individual does not always improve the organization, and good processes do not always lead to agility. Learning is important but it is only part of the solution to a major disruption in the marketplace. We may have to move closer to home to be able to resolve that contradiction.

The problem with the trajectory from unconscious incompetence to conscious incompetence to conscious competence and finally to the nirvana of unconscious competence, is that it implies a static environment. In truth, we need to focus down on being always conscious of what and why we do not know and understand the context for our current expertise. This helps us shift perspective and change belief system if the outside environment demands this. We are always striving to become competent and adapt to the changing environment. And it is the striving that is important, alongside the recognition that the ground will always be taken from underneath our feet. That striving is the essence of why learning is important. Garratt is perhaps too one dimensional in his analysis. However valuable the three-level model is, it does not explain everything or give us the whole picture.

Polaroid and sensitivity to change in the external environment

The Polaroid company, for example, was full of extraordinarily talented chemists led by Dr Edwin Land (Bonanos, 2012). Having developed a successful technology based on complex chemistry that allowed self-developing photographs to be taken, the company grew rich and prosperous. Everybody knew what a polaroid was, and the cameras and film became increasingly cheap and available to all. Yet the company, as digital technologies were emerging, single-mindedly pursued the dream of creating the world's first self-developing movie film and camera that would enable the user to shoot a roll of film and then play it back within minutes. This expensive technical breakthrough was achieved and eventually was brought to market.

The only problem was that the entire company appeared to be unaware, through ignorance or blindness, of the fast-emerging digital video technology sector. By the time the Land movie camera was brought to market, you could buy a DVI camera for a fraction of the cost, which could record almost unlimited footage that could be played back and edited instantly, making use of the evolving digital ecology of broadband, wi-fi, laptop and sophisticated editing software. The company simply did not know what they did not know, and as a consequence lost contact with the customer and the market. The launch was a disaster.

In spite of technical brilliance and devotion to the task, Edwin Land's focus on chemistry as the only solution to capturing images failed to spot the imminent side-lining of those processes. The entire company paid the price for that short-sightedness. Land was a chemist and employed chemists. He insisted that capturing images – both static and moving – required analogue film and sophisticated chemistry. He could see no other possibility; capturing images was a chemical process until the moment when that was no longer true. Then the company failed.

From making the cover of *Time* magazine in 1972, to the collapse of his company in the 2000s, his is a history of innovation and spectacular growth, followed by an equally spectacular collapse. For example, in the '70s, photographers were shooting one billion polaroid photographs a year, and polaroid became a $2 billion turnover operation with very high profit margins. It was reduced to a shell company that went bankrupt twice and was sold three times between 2003 and 2009 (Bonanos, 2012: 7). Nostalgia, coupled with an analogue photography revival, has ensured the survival of the company but as a shadow of what it once was. You can blame the hubris of Dr Edwin Land for the company's blindness, but that is only one part of the problem. Some recent research by the Corporate Research Forum – a London-based membership network organization that brings a research base to contemporary business issues – may help here.

Learning and agility

CRF published their research report on 'Learning: The Foundation for Agility and Sustainable Performance' in June 2017 (Pillans, 2017). It is based on the results of a survey of over 200 companies in their membership base. This report makes a strong business case for learning in the context of today's volatile environment. Eight-nine per cent of the organizations polled felt that learning was critical to achieving business objectives, and 96 per cent saw learning, in theory at least, as a source of competitive advantage.

When asked, however, if learning was actually a source of competitive advantage in their organization, that figure dropped to 64 per cent, and those that felt learning was not a source of competitive advantage went from 1 per cent in theory, up to 31 per cent when considering their own organization. There is still dubiety about the role and impact of learning.

The nub of the issue is in a comment in the report by Michael Chavez, the CEO of Duke Corporate Education:

> In the past 15 years, whilst the field of leadership development has become more crowded, complex and option-rich, the fundamental issue remains the same: learning and the practice of leadership development need to take an exponential leap to help the business to achieve results. I'll go a step further: the learning function must stop thinking of itself as 'supporting' the business and start thinking of itself as part of the business. (Pillans, 2017: 8)

The dilemma of the learning operation inside, and separate from the business, is that it focuses on making the organization more effective and productive in its current context, not necessarily more agile or sensitive to those critical weak signals from the outside environment. Polaroid's chemists were exceptional and leading edge, but that was not – ultimately – the point. You could argue that much of the investment in learning is about reinforcing the status quo and working on the here and now. This is essentially a reactive and responsive model rather than one that adapts to the environment and helps others adapt. Learning for the present needs to be combined with learning for the future.

At this time of turbulence and disruption on every front, Charles Darwin's percipient ideas are echoed constantly. This is not a quotation from *On the Origin of Species*, although it is widely claimed to be (see the Cambridge University site that offers a detailed analysis at www.darwinproject.ac.uk/evolution-misquotation), but a paraphrase of Darwin by Leon C Megginson in an article from 1963 on 'Lessons from Europe for American Business': 'According to Darwin's Origin of Species, it is not the most intellectual of the species that survives; it is not the strongest that survives; but the species that survives is the one that is able best to adapt and adjust to the changing environment in which it finds itself' (Megginson, 1963).

In a climate where business needs adaptive learning systems, we still roll out largely responsive and disconnected models. Garratt's three circles did attempt to emphasize the need for adaptive systems and the importance of connection with the market and, in that sense, was future facing in his endeavours. In the present, however, there is still a huge focus on making learning efficient without looking at making it truly effective.

In the CRF Report, Pillans creates a simple four-box matrix to show how learning can meet the needs of contemporary business by increasing both productive learning and generative learning for the individual employee and the organization.

The matrix looks at the learning needs of the individual and the organization at two levels: the productive and the generative. You can also look at the two levels as building excellence and competence in the present, and addressing future needs and processes that can

Figure 3.2   Pillans' matrix

	Productive	**Generative**
Working on the organization	**Organizational/Productive** Working in teams on increasing efficiency or productivity in the existing business. Examples include: • after-action reviews • delivering management training on a social learning platform • quality circles and application of other team-based continuous improvement methodologies.	**Organizational/Generative** Using the collective wisdom of the team or organization to come up with new solutions, identify new markets, and challenge existing assumptions. Examples include: • convening groups to identify the top 10 emerging disruptive innovations in your market and work out how they might affect your business model • online strategy 'jams' • co-creation through action learning.
Working on the individual	**Individual/Productive** Learning that's focused on helping an individual improve performance in their role. Examples include: • sales training • watching a video on how to manage a difficult conversation with a team member.	**Individual/Generative** Helping individuals learn key skills to enable them to generate new ideas or strategies. Examples include: • teaching people critical thinking or strategic modelling skills • teaching individuals design thinking methods.

anticipate and meet future challenges. In other words, concentrating on excellence in the present, and agility in the future. Neither approach is optional.

At the productive level, the individual learns the skills and competences to do their job. At this level, performance support as well as what is called underpinning competence are critical. This incorporates both hard skills as well as soft skills. At the organizational level, productive development includes team building, working in quality systems such as Six Sigma, or helping staff get the best from enterprise-level software that has been introduced. Building and disseminating and maintaining the organizational culture are also important.

At the generative level for the individual, mindset change and new skills such as critical thinking and systems thinking could be included alongside, for example, processes to encourage innovation and share ideas. At the organizational level, big cultural shifts can be elaborated, and the organization builds for the future, for example, with ideas jams or innovation competitions.

This is why GE set up its Destroy Your Business exercises in the 1990s, where key staff were given time to go away and work out how they could set up a new company that would effectively disrupt, and ultimately destroy the GE business in which they worked. Once these potential threats were analysed, GE then took steps to avoid such disruption (Ashkenas, 2012). So there was a practical outcome but also significant process outcomes. Staff working together intensely to analyse their external environment and determine potential threats to the business before those threats became significant, was a mindset-changing learning experience. That one-off process was designed to become a way of working that was core for leadership roles.

Garratt misses the need to evolve the learning organization inside the company and consciously build generative skill sets and processes. But he does understand the culture that is necessary to build and sustain a learning organization. The climate inside must be conducive to building generative learning skills, and there have to be processes that can act upon intelligence from outside the organization and take decisive action inside.

The final weakness of the Garratt approach is that he speaks little about building workforce engagement as a critical prerequisite for developing a learning organization. This is one of the most elemental conditions for learning to take root and flourish. It is hard to imagine disengaged or disenchanted staff being able to, or wanting to, focus on their development and the survival of their organization with any kind of enthusiasm. It is also hard to image how they will work co-operatively and innovate.

And the issue of disengagement will not go away. The Workforce Analysis by Gallup that has been in play for over 15 years shows little improvement. The headline summary of the 2017 report is that only 33 per cent of the American workforce are engaged at work, yet in the best organizations this figure rises to over 70 per cent. Similar surveys from around the world have similar conclusions.

In the Foreword, Gallup's Chairman and CEO Jim Clifton points the finger at the prevailing American leadership philosophy that he claims no longer works. His solution is to transform workplace culture and he elaborates on six core actions to build engagement. He argues that there is a crisis, and the key way forward is make workplaces think differently about their people, and to help, as a priority, their staff feel valued and concentrate on extending their capability. I would argue that a learning culture emerges from this process, and its existence is the fundamental indicator of its success.

Conclusions

This chapter is a starting place to help you think about your own organization and where you might start on the journey of transformation. It is designed to help define the kind of workplace culture you need and defines some of the criteria for developing more engaged staff and a more participative and open workplace. It focuses on building the processes that help individuals grow and develop, and how it is possible to utilize that increased skill and knowledge in individuals as a way of increasing the effectiveness of the organization as a whole. This would appear to be the only way of keeping the workplace relevant and aligned with its market and customers.

The chapter makes a powerful argument for getting the organization to talk to itself, and to drive in intelligence and insight from outside. This process is designed to keep the wider strategy on track and to act as a temperature check on the exterior and interior climate as well as help define the overall purpose: why are we here and what are we doing? The conclusion is, however, that these processes are needed but not sufficient to generate the changes they promise or build sufficient engagement in the workforce.

Garratt and Senge

In Stanford Professor Jeffrey Pfeffer's book *Leadership BS*, published in 2015, he cites the examples of corruption and failure in organizations as evidence that leaders are failing their companies on an 'almost unimaginably vast' scale (Pfeffer, 2015: 8). Increasing opportunities to learn does not appear to build organizations that are, in Garry Hamel's (2007) words, 'fit for people'. Pfeffer's book is subtitled *Fixing workplaces and careers one truth at a time*. The context for the book is, in Pfeffer's own words, 'leadership failure and career derailment'. Too many toxic 'workplaces filled with disengaged, dissatisfied employees' (Pfeffer, 2015: 16). This was not the legacy that Garratt had intended.

The current work environment is described by Josh Bersin, the Deloitte analyst, as challenging (Bersin, 2017). He describes the modern worker as being overwhelmed, with 41 per cent of time being spent on processes that give little satisfaction and do not help the work flow. That person is also distracted, constantly switching on a smartphone and going online for information and solutions, and being distracted by email, video clips and apps. Workers, he claims, are interrupted every five minutes by work applications and collaboration tools. They are also impatient as a result of being overwhelmed and distracted. Modern workers will not watch videos for longer than four minutes and will click away from any site in between 5 and 10 seconds if their attention has not been grabbed. Bersin's research and analysis reveals that the average employee has only 1 per cent of a typical workweek available to focus on their development needs; that is around 24 minutes.

In response, Bersin says that learning has to be available on any device in any place, on-demand, collaborative and immediately empowering to have any chance of making an impact. Garratt is not able to address this dilemma and did not foresee this kind of blockage to learning.

What can we learn from Senge and Garratt?

1 The concept of the learning organization is far from dead. It is a rich seam of investigation and exploration. However, what is equally clear is that Senge and Garratt do not have all the answers.

2 Garratt is too one-dimensional in his analysis. However valuable the three-level model is, it does not deal with the whole picture. Senge, on the other hand, is too complex. It is almost impossible to know where to start with his five disciplines, seven disabilities and 11 laws. He offers rich insight and his book is still valuable and insightful but confusing.

3 The unifying principle of double-loop learning endures magnificently across time. It is as relevant for individuals as it is for organizations and is simple to grasp and powerful to apply. That must be at the heart of the learning organization.

4 Returning to the thinking of the 1980s, which includes the work of Edwards Deming and Argyris, reveals the common roots for the two books. They were on to something important, and both of those thinkers changed the way companies behaved, Modern-day manufacturing owes much to Deming's pioneer work on quality improvement, and managing complex systems owes much to Argyris. In some ways, their thinking endures with more resilience than the two books that were influenced by those thinkers.

5 Understanding how complex environments work is still profoundly relevant and perhaps we need to revive systems thinking as a tool for today.

6 The complexity of learning that the two books imply goes way beyond some of the offering from L&D in modern organizations.

7 The need to focus on productive learning for today and generative learning for tomorrow, which emerges from the CRF report (Pillans, 2017), is a very helpful way of describing complex learning from organizations, and shapes some useful ideas going forward.

8 There is still much to be discovered about the nature of learning organizations, but it is a rich and relevant seam to explore as it appears to connect learning with problem solving and idea generation. It also outlines the core skills required to lead a modern organization. The concept of a learning organization says something helpful about how to deal with uncertainty and complexity. These are core ideas and spill out from the concerns of L&D alone.

Key learning

1 No organization can survive in the current climate without a strong focus on increasing the capability of all its staff.

2 All communication must be sideways as well as up and down through the organization. Silos inhibit innovation and efficiency. Increasingly the view from outside (a fundamental requirement for customer engagement) is joined up, and shared across the organization so that it becomes a holistic process with many perspectives.

3 Vigilance is required to maintain a strong connection with customers and to monitor what is happening outside the business. Disruption can happen fast and can have devastating consequences.

4 Organizations are organic and complex. They cannot be treated like machines, to be tuned or disassembled and reassembled at will.

5 Learning is holistic. A key added dimension that emerges from the learning is engagement and a propensity to share. The aim should be a workplace that is a hubbub of ideas, insight and curiosity or the organization will stall.

6 A culture of openness is required in order that sharing can occur, mistakes are admitted to and learning can flourish across the organization.

7 This process never stops. You are always aspiring to become a learning organization. The speed of change in the outside environment means that the internal churn of ideas is constant and you get better and better at dealing with them.

8 The best leaders are those that listen, not just talk. And that listening is inside the organization as well as outside the organization.

9 Developing a habit of endless curiosity coupled with the ability to pause and reflect are key attributes for knowledge workers. And there has to be an open admission of what you know and what you do not know, and where the organization is strong and where it is weak.

10 This process is self-perpetuating. When you begin to get it right, it continues to get better.

References

Ashkenas, R (2012) Kill your business model before it kills you, *Harvard Business Review*, 2 October 2012

Bersin, J (2017) 'Meet the Modern Learner', infographic at Bersin.com: www.bersin.com/uploadedFiles/112614_TL_MeetModernLearner(Info)_DJ_Final.pdf

Bonanos, C (2012) *Instant: The story of Polaroid*, Princeton Architectural Press, Princeton

Ehrlich, P R and Raven, P H (1964) Butterflies and plants: a study in coevolution, *Evolution* **18** (4) pp 586–608

Garratt, B (1987) Learning is the core of organisational survival: action learning is the key integrating process, *Journal of Management Development,* **6** (2), pp 38–44

Garratt, B (2000) *The Learning Organization*, Harper Collins, London

Garratt, B (2000) *The Twelve Organizational Capabilities: Valuing people at work,* Harper Collins, London

Garvin, D (1993) Building a learning organization, *Harvard Business Review*, July–August 1993

GE Annual Report 2000, p 4 in a section 'Relishing Change'

Hamel, G (2007) *The Future of Management*, Harvard Business School Press, Boston

Hammer, M (1990) Reengineering work: don't automate, obliterate, *Harvard Business Review*, July–August 1990, pp 104–112

Mant, A (1997) *Intelligent Leadership*, Allen and Unwin, St Leonards

Megginson, L (1963) Lessons from Europe for America, *Southwestern Social Science Quarterly*, 44 (1), pp 3–13, at p 4

Paine, N (2017) *Building Leadership Development Programmes: Zero-cost to high-investment programmes that work*, Kogan Page, London

Pfeffer, J (2015) *Leadership BS: Fixing workplaces and careers one truth at a time*, Harper Collins, New York

Pillans, G (2017) *Learning: The foundation for agility and sustainable performance*, CRF, London

Reeves, M (2015) *Your Strategy needs a Strategy: How to choose and execute the right approach*, Harvard Business Review Press, Harvard

Savitz, A (2013) *The Triple Bottom Line*, John Wiley and Sons, New Jersey

State of the American Workforce Report (2017) Gallup Inc.

William Thomas, C (2002) The rise and fall of Enron, *The Journal of Accountancy*, 1 April

What are
the core components
of a learning culture?

04

Introduction

This chapter sets out to explore the concept of a learning culture in more detail and with a wide frame of reference. It demonstrates that the component parts are rich and varied and shows how many writers have made a significant contribution. Not all of them explicitly refer to the idea of a learning culture but their insights help us flesh out the picture and deepen the exploration.

We start by looking at collaboration and a collaborative culture and the practical steps that you can take to increase the level of collaboration, by understanding its key components and the blockers. The US academic, Keith Sawyer, sees group flow (based on the idea of flow developed by the psychologist Mihaly Csikszentmihalyi in the 1990s) as the high-water mark of collaboration and the key indicator of what he calls 'group genius' (Sawyer, 2017). It is clear that there is a direct link back to Edwards Deming and his 14-point vision about how organizations should operate. Quality comes from collaboration and operating without fear. This vision was Deming's driving principle from the 1950s but it was not published until 1982. The chapter then illustrates how these ideas are embedded in successful organizations, taking SUN Microsystems, LinkedIn and Degreed as examples linked by the trajectory of Kelly Palmer's career as an impressive CLO. Kelly shows that a powerful tenet such as LinkedIn's 'transformation of the company, yourself and the world' cannot be accomplished by mere words. The entire organization has to be built around the delivery of that brave and ambitious purpose.

The chapter concludes with a discussion of trust. Trust appears everywhere in learning cultures. It is both an aspiration and a product of that culture and the first requirement before mistakes can be admitted and learning shared. It is a starting point and ending point for engagement, self-belief and extraordinary achievement.

Part 1: What are the key components of a learning culture?

The case studies in this book share the stories of very different companies, located in different parts of the world, and with very different aspirations and missions. What links them is their success, which is based, to a significant extent, on an embracing of an extensive and deep-rooted learning culture. This element draws them together and means that they share a number of common features that are described in this chapter. These are the broad, core components of a learning culture and they are indivisible. Each company exhibits all of these traits and together they define the foundation of their respective learning cultures.

The first aspect is that each company shares a strong mission, vision and values. All the organizations discussed are values driven, and the values extend from their mission and purpose. The mission is aspirational, and the values are clear, living statements of expected behaviours rather than abstract concepts. These organizations demonstrate a strong collaborative culture and are committed to innovating at all points in their value chain. Finally, they are all high-trust organizations; trust is the glue that holds the organizations together and is one of the fundamental indicators that determines how staff work together and how the companies work with their customers and suppliers.

I have extracted those common features from the case studies and elaborated on them with the help of a number of experts. For collaboration I worked with Rod Willis, who runs a research-based consultancy, Assentire, which promotes and develops collaboration and innovation in organizations, and Keith Sawyer, who researches collaboration and creativity and made specific reference to his 2007 book, *Group Genius: The creative power of collaboration* (Sawyer, 2007).

I then spoke to Kelly Palmer. She is currently the Chief Learning Officer of an Educational Technology start-up called Degreed. Degreed bills itself as a lifelong learning platform and uses artificial intelligence to curate relevant material for individuals to learn and build their skills. At an organizational level it registers the accumulative power of that skill development across the organization and allows the company to set learning goals and challenges for its staff. This company is one of the key players in a new form of learning management and delivery system. These new online environments are called 'experience platforms' and represent a different approach to storing, curating and organizing learning experiences for individuals or across whole companies. The analogy, developed first by Josh Bersin, is that these platforms are like a Netflix for learning, in terms of their attractive interfaces, algorithms that learn how and what the user learns and cumulative insight into what the users want, alongside records of what the users and their organizations have achieved.

Finally I spoke with Julian Stodd about his year-long research project on 'trust inside organizations'. He explored the parameters of trust, the degree to which trust plays a role in organizational performance as well as its significance as an enabler of innovation and staff engagement. I also talk about Stephen M R Covey's 2006 book, *The Speed of Trust: The one thing that changes everything* (Covey, 2006), which ignited a debate about the extent of trust in contemporary organizations and the linkage of trust to productivity and performance.

Collaboration and innovation

Discussion with Rod Willis, co-founder of Assentire

Rod Willis is a former engineer who has built his career around developing more collaborative working practices inside workplaces in order to make them more effective and deliver higher productivity and business impact. This work has been refined and systematized into a framework that has been promoted via Assentire Ltd. This is a business that integrates 'design thinking', with 'continuous improvement' and 'agile learning' strategies and practices to bring about lasting behavioural change across organizations.

Willis's original research indicated the importance of collaboration. It showed that more effective and extensive collaboration led to better conversations, faster problem solving and increased innovation. This was because knowledge is shared, ideas flow more fluidly, and the increase in trust that ensued meant that problems were tackled, new ideas emerged, and innovative practices were deployed more holistically.

Willis believes that there is a correlation between collaboration and an effective learning culture. A learning culture is both a by-product and an essential component of deep and effective collaboration. This is between individuals, across departments and different geographical locations. It allows staff to work better together more successfully and maximizes the reach and impact of the organization. For Willis, effective collaboration is the key to building better workplaces.

The origins of this approach and philosophy can be traced back to the quality improvement methodology developed by the US visionary W Edwards Deming, who worked hard to restore Japanese industry after the Second World War. This transformation of Japanese manufacturing after the Second World War slowly became the norm for all countries. It became known as total quality management, or TQM, and Deming is acknowledged as its father, although he never used that precise terminology. Deming incorporated a statistical approach to quality, so workers knew precisely what they were working with, and could therefore direct their energy towards developing processes to eliminate errors. The aim was to create an environment where zero defects production was a realistic aspiration, and operational excellence was the norm. In other words, quality was built, in not selected out. He moved accountability onto the line workers to get it right, rather than an army of quality control staff to check and throw out products that were sub-standard. This philosophy placed clear accountability on the line worker, who not only checked the quality of what he or she did individually, but also worked closely with colleagues in small teams to eliminate faults in the production or service process in their section. If every team covering every element of the production process did the same, products were produced with zero defects. This process required a coherent philosophy of management and Deming articulated this into 14 laws about management that were first codified in a 1982 book, *Out of the Crisis* (Deming, 1982). He never changed these laws throughout his lifetime.

If we look at Deming's 14 statements, it is clear that they are as much about organizational culture as they are about manufacturing processes (first elaborated in Deming, 1982). The points are clear principles of a strong management philosophy and their subsequent behaviours, and act as the fundamental building blocks of Deming's vision for organizations. Adhering to these laws is a necessary precursor to excellence but not sufficient in itself to move an organization forward to the next level. For Deming, innovation, quality production and efficiency are all connected to a culture of collaboration and respect for the workforce. Learning has to be an integral part of that process and a key constituent of work. Deming believed that workers should not check their brains in at reception but use their skill and knowledge to make everything better on a continuing basis. The fact that Deming was propagating this philosophy in the 1950s is a remarkable tribute to his vision and tenacity.

In an article published in 1994, Senge links Japanese industry's success to its commitment to learning and pays explicit tribute to Edwards Deming and his work in Japan:

> As management practices in Japan have evolved over the past 40 years, there has been a steady spread of the commitment to learning – starting with statistical process control (SPC) for small groups of quality experts, to teaching quality improvement tools to frontline workers throughout the organization, to developing and disseminating tools for managerial learning. (Senge, 1994)

In this article, Senge links Deming's work on quality improvement to the need for continuous learning. He sees this as the spark that ignited the idea of the learning organization.

Deming's 14 points underpin Willis's concept of collaboration. Listing them in full shows the scope and reach of Deming's vision. They concern leadership, organizational culture, trust and lifelong learning. Together they present a holistic view of how organizations should operate. It is very clear, from reading the list, what Deming saw as the key drivers for a modern, successful organization. They are written as a series of exhortations:

- Create consistency of purpose for improving products and services.
- Adopt the new philosophy.
- Cease dependence on inspection to achieve quality.
- End the practice of awarding business on price alone; instead minimize total cost by working with a single supplier.
- Improve constantly and forever every process for planning, production and service.
- Institute training on the job.
- Adopt and institute leadership.
- Drive out fear.
- Break down barriers between staff areas.
- Eliminate slogans, exhortations and targets for the workforce.
- Eliminate numerical quotas for the workforce and numerical goals for management.
- Remove barriers that rob people of pride of workmanship and eliminate the annual rating or merit system.
- Institute a vigorous programme of education and self-improvement for everyone.
- Put everybody in the company to work accomplishing transformation.

They resonate and sound contemporary now, but when they were first articulated – nearly 70 years ago – in the 1950s these ideas were revolutionary and unacceptable to many running post-war industry in the United States and Europe. This was one of the reasons why Deming went to Japan to put his ideas into practice. There he had a voice that was not always heard in contemporary US or European industry.

Today, much of his philosophy is simply part of the way in which much business is conducted. The term TQM has evolved into Continuous Improvement and more recently Operational Excellence. It is accepted as good practice in manufacturing as well as in many service industries worldwide. Indeed, during the 1980s, every developed country made pilgrimages to Japan to try and learn how it was done, and Deming was lifted out of obscurity to be fêted as the father of modern manufacturing. By this time Deming was in his 80s and enjoyed this swan song until his death at the age of 93 in 1993. He wrote and spoke widely, almost up until his death, and built up an entirely new generation of supporters.

The simple observation that Deming made over 55 years ago is that it is much slower and more expensive to inspect defects out of a process than it is to build quality in from the start. This is now widely accepted. To do this requires skill, pride and ownership of the entire workforce. This can only be achieved by highly motivated, engaged and well-trained, skilled individuals who operate within a culture of what he calls 'vigorous self-improvement' that we would now call a culture of lifelong learning.

Beyond that, Deming had a holistic vision of work places, and believed that a single consistency of purpose for everybody would engender profound respect and collaboration right through the organization from board to shop floor. This vision of collaboration did not stop at the doors of the institution but extended from the workplace to their suppliers and their customers. His idea was that a single supplier for each element of manufacture should be selected, rather than a plethora of suppliers competing on price. This committed the organization to working collaboratively with that supplier, over time, to reduce cost and increase quality. This model has been widely adopted and was one of the significant changes that Goshn's team implemented in their turnaround of Nissan (see Chapter 9). Essentially it requires extensive partnership development and trust both inside and outside the organization. The more that was realized, the greater the performance.

He also believed that forcing people into numerical targets and quotas revealed a fundamental lack of trust and increased the level of fear. It also encouraged staff, at every level, to focus on the wrong thing: meeting targets, not making great products. You had to trust everybody to make an organization successful, and the leader's job was to enable and support that process. These ideas remain fresh and relevant today.

In Deming's last publication, published in the year of his death (*The New Economics for Industry, Government, Education*) he introduced a System Model called SoPK (Deming, 1993). SoPK highlighted the need to be aware of at least four domains:

1 The domain of statistics and variation (special cause and common cause).

2 The domain of systems thinking.

3 The theory of knowledge (knowledge is neither complete nor built on established assumptions).

4 Psychology (highlighting the human component is core to any organization's performance).

Essentially it takes on the mantel of the 14 points presented in *Out of the Crisis* and details the system of transformation required to introduce a model of cooperation to replace the old, inefficient model of competition and thereby building long-term economic success.

The resistance to Deming's ideas is, according to Willis, a mindset problem created by the dominance of command and control as the principle approach to running organizations. If you instil a culture that involves telling people what to do, you inhibit potential and performance.

This naturally leads to a culture where no one is trusted to do the right thing. This ensures that complex and costly frameworks for checking and monitoring have to be established. In a recent communication with a bank, I discovered that the software used to monitor the call centre staff was faulty, and claimed staff were 'idle' when they were checking information or consulting other databases. In spite of knowing this, supervisors would routinely pull out the software records and reprimand staff for too much downtime. The result was that staff tried to game the system to avoid the criticism. Much time was wasted on everyone's behalf and zero trust existed, with a concomitant lack of engagement.

Willis (2012) and many others have argued that organizations that assume that there is a leadership group who command, and a majority who are controlled, with limited scope for autonomous action, build the antithesis of a learning organization (Paine, 2014). This model divides and fragments the workforce, which in turn diminishes both the quality and sophistication of output.

At the heart of this command and control approach is a philosophy of learning based on transmission. In other words, those who know the answers tell other people what to do. This is controlling and limiting, rather than sharing knowledge. The problem with this approach is that in our complex and uncertain environment, one-way transmission is problematic. More sophisticated kinds of learning are required, where admitting that you do not know something is acceptable, and exploration of problems and wide consultation are more normative (Klein, 1998).

This is precisely the view of learning that Chris Argyris described in his concept of double-loop learning (Argyris and Schön, 1978; see also Mark Easterly-Smith et al, 2004). This is discussed in greater detail in Chapter 2. In essence, double-loop learning is about reflective practice and knowledge building, and is the kind of learning that underpins, as well as sustains, a learning culture.

Willis has developed an instrument that allows groups to measure the kind of culture that exists within their groups and across the organization, and how strongly each individual perceives that culture. It explores how far the dynamic operates around trust and collaboration, for example, or how far it is built around a command and control mindset. In essence, he developed seven paired terms that span the cultural divide between command and control (right hand side) and shared learning (left hand side):

- Ask *and* Tell.
- Open *and* Closed.
- Many views *and* One view.
- Collaborate *and* Manipulate.
- Understand *and* Misunderstand.
- Trust *and* Mistrust.
- Enhanced work-life quality *and* Degraded work–life quality.

The instrument is used as a prompt for discussion about the nature of the group. Each member of the group is asked to score the degree to which their organization is, for example, about 'asking' rather than 'telling', acknowledging that it is possible to have both in play within the same group at the same time. The individuals rate each item of the pair on a continuum from 0 to +10 for the first item and from 0 to -10 for the second item. For example, a high asking culture would get a high plus score and a high telling culture would be given a high negative score.

Willis has turned this process into a card game, where each individual chooses a card with what is considered to be the appropriate score and places it face down on the table. When everyone has done this, the scores are revealed simultaneously and the differences in chosen scores are discussed. The group is tasked with coming to an agreement on a single score for each item and entering it on the chart below. This chart represents the group dynamic. If the assessment is used multiple times, improvement in desired behaviour exhibited within the group can be measured, ie the score increases moving towards the upper side (see Figure 4.1).

Figure 4.1   Exploring the group dynamic

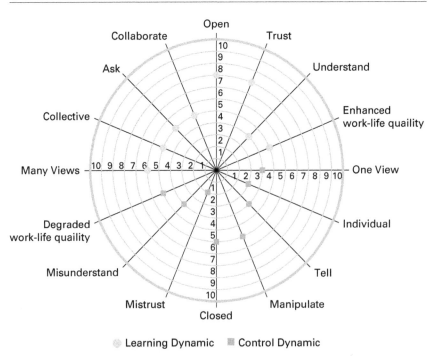

SOURCE Assentire Ltd getCoolaborating © 2017

Intrinsic and extrinsic motivation and collaboration

The less negative the score on the lower side and the more positive on the upper, the higher the readiness to collaborate. This will result in the group being more effective in its learning, problem-solving and innovation capability. There is another domain that is explored at the same time (not illustrated). Willis called this the environment dynamic. This identifies the key environmental factors that encourage intrinsic motivation and assesses the engagement of those outside of the team towards the team.

We actually learned of the concept of intrinsic motivation from research conducted in the 1950s on the puzzle-solving abilities of rhesus monkeys. This research was further developed and named Self-Determination Theory (SDT was initially developed by Deci and Ryan, 2000) and later popularized and promoted in Dan Pink's *Drive* (Pink, 2009).

What Pink argued was that motivation, based on the 1950s research and later elaborated by SDT, was based around three requirements: autonomy, mastery and purpose. These three requirements for intrinsic motivation were stronger and more effective than many extrinsic rewards. Pink quotes the research when he describes how 'It would appear that this drive... may be as basic and strong as the [other] drives. Furthermore, there is some reason to believe that [it] can be as efficient in facilitating learning' (Pink, 2009).

If you want to motivate your staff then you need to create a culture that encourages individual autonomy, the opportunity to operate to a high standard of competence; mastery and understanding the bigger picture: what do I do that fits into the ultimate aims of the organization? This is purpose. A whole organization where people who perform beyond their job description, and where there is a clear sense of purpose, almost defines a place where collaboration occurs and where knowledge is freely shared.

On the other hand, when the opposite is true and there is little autonomy, no attempt to encourage mastery and a confused or non-existent sense of purpose, there tends to be a strong resistance to change and an increase in demotivation. Willis believes his instruments (the one described above is part of a suite that he has developed) allow groups to explore the underlying culture of their own group and can be extended to the entire organization and thereby change it.

The process of scoring and filling in the segmented circle allows free discussion about key aspects of the group and encourages a group commitment to build mutual understanding as well as a more collaborative group dynamic, while better understanding its relationship with the environment they are operating within. As the process reveals the nature of the group and the organizational culture, it sets in place plans and schemes to evolve that culture into one that is more collaborative and much more of a learning environment.

The initial scoring is done individually before results are shared. This prevents group think or dominance of the loudest voice. Members can share what they really think and understand how their colleagues experience the same space. This technique is designed to allow a full and open discussion, which creates both insight about the group, the organization, as well as insight about the people around you. It is a safe way of gaining agreement and defining what needs to change, as well as helping each person understand the perspective of each of his or her colleagues. After following that process, any group should be able to work more effectively and build a more effective group dynamic.

Willis's approach to building a learning culture focuses not so much on the learning but on creating the right conditions for learning to take place. Complex and sophisticated organizations with high levels of collaboration and sharing clearly require complex and continual learning processes. Those that miss this imperative to collaborate and learn are likely to sub-optimize their own operational excellence and potential for innovation that impacts across the whole organization. An extraordinary potential blind spot!

Defining collaborative organizations

Group Genius by Keith Sawyer (Sawyer, 2007, revised edition 2017) takes a similar tack. His research puts to the sword the concept of the lone creative genius. He explores the power of collaboration to create what he calls 'group flow' and high levels of collaboration and innovation. All of this scales into the concept of the collaborative organization.

Sawyer takes his idea of group flow from the concept of flow or heightened consciousness, which was elaborated on by the psychologist Csikszentmihalyi (*Flow: The psychology of optimal experience*, 1990). *Flow* describes a state of mind where extreme focus and optimal experience are possible. It is the point where time stands still, and excellent work can be accomplished, almost effortlessly, and where the individual is completely absorbed in the experience. Sawyer's work extends the notion of flow from the individual to the group.

There are 10 conditions (Sawyer, 2007: 50–65) for group flow to occur, and they almost sketch out the way that a learning culture operates, and certainly no group flow is possible without that sharing and openness at the heart of a learning culture. The first condition is establishing a goal that is, on the one hand, enough to focus the group, but also open enough to allow improvisation and ideas to flow through. It requires some competition to stimulate creativity, but not too much to stifle original thought and original thinking. The second condition is close listening, which I refer to as active listening, and deep engagement with the team. The third is complete concentration, where there is a barrier between the group and everybody and everything else. Dan Pink's autonomy is the fourth condition where participants are in control of their actions and decisions. The need to respect the group and 'blend egos' is the fifth condition. Equal participation is the sixth condition. Rather like Vigotsky's zone of proximal development (Vigotsky, 1970), people learn and create most effectively in groups that are more or less equal. If there are too many members far in advance of the rest, they are bored, and that gap in knowledge or ability makes the others reluctant to share. Linked to that is the idea of familiarity. It is the seventh condition. If you know your team, you are more relaxed and more open with them. Good communication, which is, in effect, a blend of the third and fourth conditions, is the eighth condition. The ninth condition is 'Moving it Forward'. This is the standard methodology used in improv: always 'yes and...' rather than 'no but...' The group should always build and extend what has gone before, rather than demolish other ideas or solutions. Finally, the group has to accept and embrace the concept of failure, individually and as a group. The members need to feel safe enough to challenge each other, and willing to reject ideas or concepts that are not working.

Sawyer describes, later in the book, the concept of the collaborative organization. Here the logic of group flow is applied to the organization as a whole. He cites a number of organizations that meet his 10 criteria, which all reflect intense collaboration, trust and dense networking and extensive knowledge share.

Sawyer finishes his book with these stirring words:

> The peak state of group flow. The conversations that spark ideas, as we play off one another . The improvizational flow of a process that generates surprising and unpredictable creativity. The collaborative webs that result in innovations that are more surprising and wonderful than what any one person could create alone. That's group genius. (Sawyer, 2007: 275)

None of these conditions can be met without shared learning, trust and a strong culture of collaboration.

Part 2: Common mission, vision and purpose – a conversation with Kelly Palmer

The exploration of mission, vision and purpose and how they are critical underpinnings for a learning culture formed the core of a discussion with Kelly Palmer. Kelly has had a 30-year career in the tech industry in Silicon Valley. She lives in San Francisco and drives a Tesla, which makes her a bit of a West Coast icon! She has worked for four companies in her career that reflect the changing composition and aspiration of the tech industry. However, above all, they reflect the changing nature of work, and the critical importance of a strong learning culture to maintain innovation, and sustain the commitment and engagement of employees. They are becoming the fundamental building blocks for developing a successful business.

Kelly began her career at Sun Microsystems. Sun Microsystems ran its own version of UNIX and built workstations and servers to run their own software system. With OpenOffice and many other apps, it was a self-contained computing environment offering an extremely high-end alternative to Microsoft and Windows. Sun servers, for example, powered graphic, video and animation software, and in the early days of computer animation, for example, allowed extremely high-resolution frame rendering that virtually no other software and hardware system could deliver.

The hugely successful Silicon Valley company, which in its heyday employed 46,000 staff, had a long run in the computing industry. It was founded in 1982 by a group of Stanford University graduate students (hence the name Stanford University Network). It was profitable from its first quarter and went on until 2010 when it was acquired by the software company Oracle (https://en.m.wikipedia. org/wiki/Sun_Microsystems). Its name lives on, on the servers that Oracle now sells.

When Kelly joined Sun, it was a company of 8,000 staff, and under the leadership of Scott McNealy had become an extraordinarily innovative and creative environment in which to work and learn. Kelly had a 21-year career in Sun. She started in product development, ending up as the director of product engineering. She supported all of the software engineers and their work from back-end to user interface design, as well as training people to use that software and systems. When Sun grew and began acquiring and integrating other companies, she went with her boss into this area. He then moved to corporate strategy and she moved with him. That complex process of integrating new companies and their products required a deep product knowledge, but also commitment and interest in the human side of the business. Integrating new companies was fundamentally about integrating new staff. She helped bridge any skill deficits in the staff moving into Sun, as well as preparing them for, and integrating them into, that new corporate culture.

This process helped Kelly move from the technical and software side of the business to the people area. This is the point where she got interested in learning, and when the company created a CLO role, which was taken by Karie Willyerd who built one of the top corporate learning operations in the world, Kelly became the senior director of design and development for all learning at Sun. The company supported and encouraged her to take a Master's degree in instructional performance and technology while in that role. Eventually she built up an impressive learning organization of 150 people charged with designing and developing resources, not only for employees, but for customers and partners as well. She was located in global sales and service rather than HR and her division was created as a profit centre, which generated revenue in excess of $500 million a year. Sun did not grab these profits and put them on the bottom line but encouraged the learning organization to use that resource as investment for innovation, particularly in learning technologies.

This allowed the company to support a large learning technology team, and to be involved in constant experimentation. In trying to capture new ideas and knowledge in response to the rapid development of technology, Sun set up the SLX (Sun Learning Exchange), an online video-sharing platform that eventually evolved into a platform called Jambok. When Oracle acquired Sun in 2010, there was no interest in tech innovation or in having a big learning organization so both Karie Willyerd and Kelly left the company. Karie took Jambok with her and spun it off as a separate company. The platform continued to be developed until it was acquired by SuccessFactors in 2011. SuccessFactors was in turn acquired by SAP. Karie still works for SAP and the product is still sold by SAP as SAP Jam. The acquisition of Jambok was explored by many commentators and Josh Bersin – of Bersin Deloitte – asked in his blog of 14 March 2011: 'Is [Jambok] Corporate Learning 3.0?' (Berins, 2011).

Sun Microsystems was set up to mirror the collegiality of a college campus and recreate the spirit of enquiry and debate at Stanford University. The atmosphere was positive and collaborative. People were helpful and wanted to share and work together on problems regardless of job description or area of expertise. The organization was mercifully unencumbered by office politics and backstabbing. McNealy believed that his staff should be happy and concerned about each other, and that this would build innovation and success. Unlike most other Silicon Valley companies, layoffs were unheard of until the end of 2007 when Sun was in search of a buyer. It was, therefore, a stable environment where many staff felt privileged to work. Kelly was there at a time of hyper-growth but the culture was stable and innovative.

The whole atmosphere engendered a high level of trust. The workforce felt more like an engaged community working on whatever the company needed to be done, rather than individuals employed to fulfil one task, or one role. It did not mean that the company was perfect. It could defocus and chase too many hares at one time. For instance, Sun invented the Java programming language but never managed to develop or monetize it, in spite of its rapid uptake for web-based programming solutions.

Sun was ahead of its time in other ways too; when other companies were building self-aggrandizing HQs for themselves, Sun chose to do the opposite. In Silicon Valley, due to the geographical proximity of so many aspiring young companies, there was some competition between the companies for land, and to see who could build the most stunning buildings. For example, Sun was located across from Google in Mountain View and they competed for space at one time. However, Sun deliberately chose to go in another direction. They began closing down physical campuses in order that staff could, if they chose, work remotely using the company's own technology to facilitate this. This was popular with staff and created another unique aspect of the Sun Microsystems' culture that differentiated it from other hardware and software companies dotted down the Silicon Valley. The company pioneered an emphasis on staff work/life balance, together with a focus on output rather than merely putting in the hours in a central location.

Evidence of the success of this culture and the powerful impact that it made on its staff is provided by the continued existence of the Sun alumni group, and a continuing pride in having worked for Sun. It is now almost 10 years since its sale to Oracle and the only thing that remains of Sun Microsystems is the brand that is still displayed on all of Oracle's servers. It still stands as an indicator of power, reliability and quality, therefore a differentiator for the hardware marketplace.

There are a number of features of Sun Microsystems as an employer, which other organizations with strong learning cultures share. The first is a belief that staff should be all they can be, rather than tied to one role or one area of the business simply because that is the one into which they were recruited. The second is that hard work is important but so is having an enjoyable experience at work.

Sun Microsystems had its own expression, which was: 'kick butt, have fun'. The third is a really strong focus on collaboration, and a strong allegiance to the company as a whole, not separate divisions or separate teams. The fourth was deep respect for everybody's expertise. If you needed to know something, a colleague was the first person to turn to. Finally, there was a commitment to continue learning and play an active part in evolving the company. This made it a successful and distinctive player in the market.

Sun represented a computing paradigm that worked for over 25 years. Although it has, to all intents and purposes, disappeared, its approach and philosophy endure to this day, if only through the strong alumni group that retains the Sun spirit and continues the Sun ethos.

Kelly moved from Sun before the ink was dry on the sale to Oracle. She spent two years at Yahoo and worked alongside five different CEOs in that brief time – possibly a unique work experience. In many ways that statement sums up Yahoo at the time. It was the opposite of Sun. The company was full of disgruntled and deflated employees who had no sense of the direction of the company that no new incoming CEO could apparently instil.

She decided to move to another company in hyper-growth mode. Having been an enthusiast about the relatively young LinkedIn she secured the Chief Learning Officer role there in 2012. At the time it employed just 2,000 staff and was in the relatively early stages of Jeff Weiner's tenure as CEO, with the founder Reid Hoffman moving to a more advisory role on the board.

Weiner actually joined LinkedIn in 2008 as interim president and then moved into the CEO role shortly thereafter in 2009. LinkedIn remained relatively small until its IPO in 2011. In 2010 it had only 1,000 employees. By 2012, this had risen to 2,000 but in 2016 this had increased to over 11,000 (https://techcrunch.com/2009/06/24/changing-of-the-guard-jeff-weiner-takes-ceo-spot-at-linkedin/and https://ourstory.linkedin.com).

Kelly spent four years at LinkedIn. Its spectacular growth meant that staff had to be trusted to manage these huge transitions, so autonomy was a big part of the culture, as was innovation. What drove, and still drives LinkedIn, is their five cultural tenets and their five related values. These were almost recited as a mantra before big meetings. Staff were encouraged to embrace, endorse and live those tenets and the values. They defined the nature of the company and its consistent direction. They are not on posters or behind the reception desk but treated as living values that informed the backdrop to any critical decisions. Essentially, the performance review process at LinkedIn was a conversation about how well you were doing when judged against the company's culture and values.

LinkedIn was set up to change the world. That idea of making a difference was a key aspiration for the company and therefore a key aspiration for every single person who worked in it. In fact, 'transformation of the company, yourself and the world' is still the first cultural tenet. The second is the idea of providing opportunities for everybody – this meant LinkedIn members as well as staff. The other tenets are: integrity, collaboration, humour and finally, delivering results.

These tenets would not have been out of place in Sun Microsystems. The values in LinkedIn offered more practical and down-to-earth guidelines rather than big, aspirational ideas. These are: members first; relationships matter; be open, honest and constructive; demand excellence; take intelligent risks; and act like an owner. If any member of staff had to make a difficult decision, the values indicated the way to go, in order to make the right decision.

In that hyper-growth mode, LinkedIn went from 2,000 staff when Kelly joined to 11,000 over the four years she worked for the company. But in spite of that speed of recruitment, if anyone came to an interview and did not understand the vision or the mission, and could not articulate LinkedIn's potential impact on the world of work, they were not employed. LinkedIn wanted staff who were passionate about the company and what it could achieve. They were early adopters of the core acquisition philosophy 'recruit for attitude and develop the skills'. Kelly had the tough job of building an appropriate on-boarding programme that was able to cope with the numbers joining, while remaining true to the vision and values of the company. Everyone who came through that process knew what was expected of them and understood, and committed to, the workplace culture that they were joining.

The model for all leadership behaviours in the company was built around Fred Kofman's philosophy expounded in his best-known publication, *Conscious Business* (Kofman, 2013). The model was driven top-down in the organization and included a focus on authentic communication, responsibility, integrity and humility as well as emotional control. This leadership framework aligns well with the four key components of a learning culture and can be seen as an essential precursor to the building of a learning organization.

This framework of behaviours was not seen as interesting or desirable, but as the deep and profound core beliefs that underpinned the culture and assured the company's future. Kelly's role as CLO meant she was, in essence, the cultural champion. This was partly based on the on-boarding programme but also emerged from a philosophy of encouraging skills development and lifelong learning. The company also built access pathways for all staff to encourage career development.

Kelly focused on reimagining how learning could be structured and delivered. She drew on her extensive knowledge to implement learning technologies that could scale, rather than employing a more orthodox learning management system. The company reimagined what a learning platform might be and concentrated on delivering a simple but exceptional user experience. The company built this platform using their own small technology team. This eventually became a comprehensive learning experience called 'LearnIn'. The focus was on building a process based around engagement, exploration and opportunity rather than about building and distributing content. At the time, this was as radical as it was exciting. The core philosophy was to enable learning rather than deliver courses.

With the acquisition in 2015 of the course delivery platform Lynda.com, LinkedIn moved heavily into content development and distribution. It integrated Lynda.Com into the main LinkedIn platform as 'LinkedIn Learning'. The company started to build its own LMS to distribute this content to its staff, but also to deliver Lynda.com content to LinkedIn's members. This meant that the company could offer corporate customers a more comprehensive (and income generating) learning service. The result of this shift in focus was that the in-house learning development team was disbanded and LearnIn marginalized.

The product manager for LearnIn moved to a brand-new start-up called Degreed. This was a software platform that shared curated content and learned the user's needs and aspirations using artificial intelligence. This former staff member introduced Kelly to David Blake, the founder and CEO of Degreed and, in spite of the fact that this was a very small company with around 120 staff when she joined, Blake created the role of CLO and offered it to Kelly.

Degreed has no HR operation in the traditional sense, as the CFO handles all the functional tasks, and the talent and learning strategy is driven by Kelly. She is, in essence, the chief learning and talent officer in the organization, reporting directly to the CEO. The company therefore mirrors the approach to learning inside its own organization that it wants to drive into other companies that use the Degreed learning platform. In essence, the small team of staff in Degreed became super-users of their own platform, and act as a living case study of what Degreed can achieve and what other companies can, in turn, achieve.

The company has an extremely distributed workforce with small offices in San Francisco and Salt Lake City as well as in an increasing number of countries around the world. But most staff do not work from those offices. They work from home or from wherever they are travelling. There is no organizational chart or detailed job descriptions. Staff come together to do the work, disband, rejoin new groups and so on. They are trusted to get on and do what is necessary, to support each other, to grow and develop the company. The core operating principles are driven by what they internally call a 'Brand Bible', which lays down the company culture and its values.

Degreed's values are striking. One of the company values is to emphasize that family is more important than company. This is reflected in a relatively flat structure with a focus on flexibility and balance. The company teams concentrate on delivery and on success, not hours worked. A potentially happy family life is actively encouraged.

There are values around the idea of dedication, excellence, candour and coach-ability, alongside transparency and learning. One further aspect of the company can be summed up in the Chief Executive's expression: 'If it ends, it ends'. In other words, the company is driven by a vision that encapsulates what they want to do in the world. If they cannot execute that vision, they will not cling on, but walk away. The company is therefore built around belief and commitment rather than focusing only on survival and profit. Its mission drives commitment and loyalty and is a huge part of its strength and resilience. In this way, the learning culture is reflected in, and emerges out of, the way the company is run. The focus is on encouraging staff to build their own learning journeys in order to stay on top of their game. The software that they produce helps them on that learning journey and supports a completely open and flexible view of learning.

Degreed is not so much about creating content, its focus is more about discovering content that already exists, encouraging users to access it, learn, build skills and share it with their peers. All staff are encouraged to learn and grow. The company has skills plans and learning pathways. Staff can use these; however, they are also encouraged to follow their own passions and build their own careers. There are no formal programmes as such, but rather extended opportunities to learn and develop.

The learning culture expects (rather like the WD-40 Company) continuous learning every day. This is measured and tracked back to each member of staff's personal learning profile. Each individual owns that process but gets extensive guidance and feedback from their managers to fine tune it. There are encouraged to recommend content to their peers, and there are leaderboards linked to the skill plan mastery. For example, the role of CLO has 10 skills listed. Kelly's job is to track her own progress and encourage peer review to help her work out what she still needs to do to meet that skill profile.

Degreed also has a feature called Flex-Ed that allots employees a certain dollar amount per year to spend on their own learning as they see fit. Currently each employee receives $100/month or $1200/year to spend on whatever learning they want. It can be a book or online course, in-person class or event.

Other Degreed customers have used this as well, and it not only gives employees the opportunity to learn how and what they like, but it also releases to the organization the data to know what people are learning. The company is heavily data-driven, using analytics to tell the learning story rather than relying on guesswork or happenstance.

Organizations increasingly want to know what their employees are learning and what skills they are building, and Degreed's data analytics allows them to see that in terms of all the learning they do, both formal and informal. These data patterns are continuously shared around the organization. Degreed believes in the power of a learning culture to keep a company on track. This data is one of the ways that a company can better understand the needs of its customers. Degreed adjusts its platform on a regular basis to meet those emerging needs.

There is a sense that the very core values of Sun, to work hard but have fun, have been handed down to a contemporary organization. In Degreed, the CEO urges everyone to be as passionate as he is about the mission of the company, as well as build their own skills and profile in order to have successful careers. He wants people to remain who really want to be in the company, but he also wants people to know when it is time to move on. Every person employed is asked to sign up to that mission and take on the responsibility of being an enthusiastic learner, sharing some of that enthusiasm with customers, suppliers and fellow workers. It is an exciting perspective on a learning culture at work.

Part 3: The core underpinning process: trust – a conversation with Julian Stodd

The centrality of trust reoccurs in interviews with companies that have strong learning cultures and individuals who have built learning cultures. In essence, trust mandates organizations to offer their staff a degree of autonomy, and help them achieve mastery while building a strong sense of purpose. These are the three drivers for motivation and engagement most clearly expounded in Daniel Pink's bestselling book, *Drive*. The issue of trust, however, goes much further than that. It is the driving logic at the heart of Stephen Covey's 2006 book, *The Speed of Trust*.

Trust it is a dominant behaviour in companies with an advanced learning culture. It manifests itself in the relationship between individual employees, but it resonates as a behaviour across the organization as a whole and with customers and suppliers. What this means is that decisions can be taken rapidly with a minimum of checking and cross-referencing. This is why Stephen Covey chose to call his book *The Speed of Trust*. His thesis is that a high-trust culture speeds up the way business is conducted and lowers costs. The impact and importance of trust is the basis for Julian Stodd's detailed research project on the nature of trust in contemporary organizations and much of what he has found aligns heavily with Covey in terms of its importance and impact (Stodd, 2017).

Covey defines the span of trust in an organization across five waves. The first concerns the individual and therefore focuses on their credibility, integrity and capability. Individuals that are highly capable and have credibility inside and outside the workplace are richly prized, but Covey would add that behaving with integrity is an equally important trait. His second wave is about relationships. There he defines 13 behaviours that build and extend trust, such as 'talk straight', 'clarify expectations' and 'keep commitments'. These are extensions of individual integrity stretched across the workplace as a whole and into relationships with customers and stakeholders. They are the defining behaviours that describe and inform the overall culture of an organization. Therefore you can say that an employer has integrity as well as the staff have integrity. This is Covey's third wave. The third wave describes trust inside and across the organization. Covey defines this as alignment. In other words, everyone is facing in the same direction. The integrity of the individual is matched by the quality of the relationships within the workplace, and between the workplace and its core stakeholders.

The fourth and fifth waves are about stakeholder trust. Market trust is the fourth wave. This is all about how the outside world views an organization and judges its reputation. The fifth wave concerns societal trust: how a company behaves in its community, and how it impacts on the world as a whole. It goes beyond products and profit and loss and looks at the bigger picture. This he calls, 'the principal of contribution'.

These interlocking circles from individual integrity to community contribution are illustrated in Figure 4.2.

Covey, however, is not a naïve believer in extending trust with abandon. His analysis focuses on smart trust, rather than blind trust.

Figure 4.2   Five waves: The span of trust in an organization

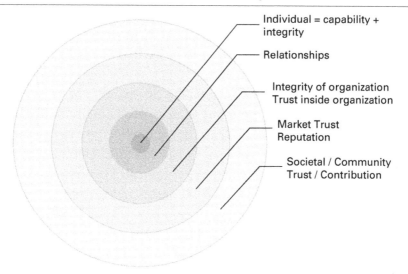

Individual = capability + integrity

Relationships

Integrity of organization
Trust inside organization

Market Trust
Reputation

Societal / Community
Trust / Contribution

He clarifies the difference in an illustration. The curve that Covey describes starts with distrust and suspicion (Covey, 2006: 287). It moves into smart trust, which involves judgement, and then falls again with blind trust that demonstrates gullibility. The aim of the book is to help organizations hit the sweet spot, and avoid either a culture of distrust and suspicion, or one of blind trust and gullibility. It is, essentially, a propensity to trust, based on detailed analysis and constant awareness. Trust is always built slowly; however, it can be destroyed in an instant.

The key is to extend trust gradually, and reinforce the process constantly at the individual, the relationship, as well as the organizational level. Covey would argue that trust is a holistic process. If you see a company's reputation ruined in the marketplace, an organization betraying its community, or attempting to get away with illegal behaviour, this can be traced back to the integrity of individual staff and the way that those staff behave towards each other and towards their customers. A company that behaves badly will be a low-trust organization. It will demonstrate few, if any, of the 13 expected behaviours that Covey lists, ie no straight talking and no willingness to keep commitments and so on.

Julian Stodd, the founder of SeaSalt Learning and a well-known commentator on social leadership, is in the process of running a major research project on trust, which he calls 'The Landscape of Trust' (Stodd, 2017). His landscape is similar to Covey's in that it includes the individual, peer-to-peer trust, organizational trust as well as trust in communities. He adds as his fourth pillar the concept of trust in technology (Figure 4.3).

His research is set in three phases. The first phase is based on gathering narratives from a thousand sources. He is interviewing large numbers of people by questionnaire and a smaller number in face-to-face encounters. Finally, LinkedIn and Twitter are being used to pull in other comments from anyone who is interested in the concept. The questions are focused on 'what trust means to me' and stories are being gathered on how trust is built, and how trust is broken, 'where trust is held, and who it favours' (Stodd, 2017).

The second phase will build a prototype diagnostic that will be trialled by around a 1,000 people in 10 large organizations in order to try to gauge the impact that organizational culture, and even broader societal culture, has on trust. The direction of travel is clear, even if the outcomes of the project are still tentative (Stodd, 2018).

Figure 4.3

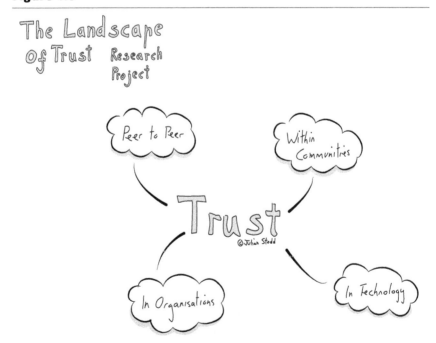

Essentially, the movement is from the individual to the organization and then back to the individual in order to map the trust aginst key behaviours. In Stodd's (2017) words:

> an individual can use [this instrument] to explore the foundation of trust, the expression of trust, and the experience of trust. These broadly relate to my intention, my action, and my impact. At the heart of these will be my individual values, which is effectively what we are exploring when we map the overall organizational landscape.

The third phase proposes to use the diagnostic to make interventions in organizations to help them understand the state of trust, and to build or rebuild high-trust environments.

Trust is a continuing and critical area of interest because it is central to creating organizations free from fear, which is the baseline for exploration, experimentation and cross-organizational learning. The fact that it is nebulous and hard to pin down does not prevent its critical role in any meaningful description of a learning culture.

Conclusions

All of the underpinning characteristic of a learning culture are manifested by all of the companies that are case studied in this book. And the message is reinforced by other work. For example, in July 2017 an article by Goran, LaBerge and Srinivasan published in the *McKinsey Quarterly*, examined how shortcomings in organizational culture have a huge impact on the economic performance of the organization and this is exacerbated and exaggerated in a digital world. The authors catalogue three negative cultural attributes in particular that emerged from a significant survey of companies. They then analyse the negative correlation between those three attributes and economic performance.

The three are: aversion to risk, siloed mindsets and behaviour, and a lack of customer focus. These three have a moderate negative impact on economic performance. This chapter has demonstrated that all three are linked, not to a lack of learning (there can be a huge amount of mandated or individual learning), but to the absence of a learning culture.

The three cultural elements reveal a lack of trust, a fear of making mistakes, or at least owning up to them, and an absence of knowledge sharing or desire to work collectively on problem solving. The power of these elements transcends the needs of the customer, and mitigates against a strong desire to provide a great customer experience. The article is headed 'culture for a digital age', and indeed the replacement of those negative cultural attributes by their opposite: risk taking, a growth mindset together with sharing across the organization, and strong customer focus are critical for survival.

This is encapsulated in a 2016 McKinsey interview with Ed Catmull, the Co-Founder of Pixar. He explained how important it is for individuals and for organizations to learn from failure and how hard that process is to establish: 'The difficulty is that when you're running an experiment, it's forward-looking. We have to try extra hard to make it safe to fail.'

In a world full of disruption and digital transformation there is huge competitive advantage for those organizations that are prepared to experiment and take small risks, and not blame each other when things go wrong. Organizations with a learning culture are far more willing to share, and more able to look openly at what did not work, and then adjust and reset with this new insight. This is an obvious attribute of the WD-40 Company, which is case studied in Chapter 5.

Organizational culture is complex; however, the current climate requires that organizations take it more seriously, as well as doing their best to adjust their culture to suit the economic and technological environment. Schein describes this trajectory across the various editions of his most famous book, *Organizational Culture and Leadership* (see Chapter 1). Starting at a point where culture was invisible and unacknowledged, and now (in the fifth edition of 2017) moving towards a point where culture is actively debated, analysed and consciously built.

The learning aspect becomes, as I have described elsewhere in this book (see Chapter 1), a sensitive gyroscope that can ensure that the organizational culture as a whole continues to align with the external environment. A learning culture also ensures that individuals are supported in the transition and helped to move forward. In a case study of the Dutch Bank ING that McKinsey also published in 2017, 'dealing with knowledge' is a critical performance metric. Peter Jacobs, ING's CIO, explains that in the agile performance-management model that ING established, 'there are no projects as such; what matters is how people deal with knowledge. A big part of the transformation has been about ensuring there is a good mix between different layers of knowledge and expertise.'

In some ways the new model is exemplified in ING by the way the teams are mixed together so that they can share knowledge more readily. In their 3,500-strong head office, former departments, such as marketing and product management, have been merged into inter-disciplinary teams that are divided into tribes and subdivided into squads. Agile coaches help managers learn how to get out of the way after setting the overall budget, direction and so on. Staff are empowered and given as much autonomy as possible. Jacobs adds:

> A lot is also down to the new way we communicate in the new office configuration. Investing in tearing down walls and buildings to create more open spaces and to allow more informal interaction between employees. We have some very small number of formal meetings; most are informal. The whole atmosphere of the organization is much more that of the tech campus than old-style traditional bank where people were locked away behind closed doors.

We are almost back, at this point, to the deliberate attempts, at Sun Microsystems in the 1980s, to recreate the campus feel of Stanford University in order to build an environment where people could freely share ideas and learn from each other.

This new openness at ING is manifested in their QBR (quarterly business reviews). Each tribe writes down what it has achieved over the last quarter, and its biggest learning, thereby celebrating both success and failure. The tribe then sets out what it intends to do in the next quarter. All of these QBRs are available for all tribes to view and to comment on, or offer support and any other input. Everything is much more transparent, and all plans are displayed on walls around the offices. It is a transformation brought about by embracing agile methodologies, but it only works when this is reflected in the culture of the organization. You have to ensure that everything, from the physical working environment to the people you sit with, aligns.

It can also involve making difficult choices. The original head office teams were reduced to 2,500 employees and they were selected on their attitude and mindset, rather than purely on knowledge and expertise. Their intrinsic capability and attitude meant that there was some enthusiasm and commitment to making the new approach work.

Behind this realignment of the company was the fundamental insight that ING was actually a technology company operating in the financial sector, rather than a bank using technology. It therefore judged its performance and organizational success against other technology companies, rather than against other banks. In some ways, therefore, ING wanted to be reviewed against companies, such as Spotify, LinkedIn and Degreed, than against other mainstream banks that have not made this leap forward. This set a very high standard, but was integral to that mindset change.

A learning culture is not sufficient in itself, nor can it ever stand alone in an organization. It is a critical building block for more open creative and digitally aware businesses. And the component parts of that learning culture appear to be increasingly indispensable elements for success in the current social and economic climate.

Key learning

1 This chapter illustrates some of the key components of a learning culture. They form both the conditions for that culture and the consequences of it.

2 The behaviours that are discussed go back to the work of Edwards Deming in the 1950s, and come right up to the recent research by McKinsey. Everything hinges on minimizing fear, developing trust and creating a climate of whole organization sharing.

3 This sequence is not new. The work of Sun Microsystems in the 1980s and its deeply embedded learning culture informed the way that contemporary organizations such as LinkedIn and Degreed aspire to behave.

4 There is no one model or one thinker that 'owns' this space. The work of Deming resonates as clearly as the thinking of Fred

Kofman. Kofman's conscious business was built on: authentic communication, responsibility, integrity and humility as well as emotional control.

They resonate well with Deming's 14 points. Those such as: adopt and institute leadership; drive out fear; break down barriers between staff areas and crucially, put everybody in the company to work accomplishing transformation. They link with Willis's collaboration framework, which celebrates, among others: many views, collaboration, understanding and trust.

5 Pink's autonomy, mastery and control can be seen as an end product of that cultural shift, as can Saywer's concept of group flow. It is all about building an environment of engaged employees who enjoy their work, are aware of their contribution and gain most fulfilment from their teams (or tribes).

6 Wrapped around the whole chapter is the concept of trust. No learning culture exists without a high degree of trust across the whole organization. It is the ultimate starting point, and the spectacular finishing point for engagement, sharing and learning.

7 Do work out the state of readiness in your organization: take a long view; take steps to build the critical elements of the culture.

8 Work out the fundamental blockers that hold your organization back and tackle them first. You discover those by asking staff and listening to the answers.

References

Argyris, C and Schön, D (1978) Organizational Learning: A theory of action perspective, Addison-Wesley Pub Co, Reading, Mass

Bersin by Deloitte Blog post, 14 March 2011: blog.bersin.com/ successfactors-acquires-jambok-is-this-corporate-learning-3-0/

Catmull, E (2016) 'Staying one step ahead at Pixar': an Interview with Ed Catmull, Mckinsey Quarterly, March 2016

Covey, S M R (2006) The Speed of Trust: The one thing that changes everything, Simon and Schuster, London

Csikszentmihalyi, M (1990) Flow: The psychology of optimal experience, Harper Perennial

Deming, W E (1982) Out of the Crisis, Preface, MIT Press

Deming, E (1993) *The New Economics for Industry, Government, Education*, MIT Press

Easterly-Smith, M, et al (2004) Constructing contributions to organizational learning: Argyris and the next generation, *Management Learning*, 35 (4), pp 371–80

Kofman, F (2013) *Conscious Business: How to build value through values*, Sounds True, Boulder, Colorado

Paine, N, (2014) *The Learning Challenge*, Kogan Page, London

Pink, D (2009) *Drive: The surprising truth about what motivates us*, Cannongate, Edinburgh

Ryan, R M and Deci, E L (2000) Self-determination theory and the facilitation of intrinsic motivation, social development, and well-being, *American Psychologist*, 55 (1), pp 68–78

Sawyer, K (2007) *Group Genius: The creative power of collaboration*, Basic Books, New York

Senge, P (1994) The learning organization, in *The Training and Development Sourcebook*, ed C E Schneier et al, p 380, Human Resource Development Press

Stodd, J (2017) Learning Blog, 13 February, 'The Landscape of Trust research project': www.julianstodd.wordpress.com

Stodd, J (2018) *The Landscape of Trust Sketchbook and Guidebook*, Sea Salt Learning, Bournemouth

Willis, R (2012) What drives resistance to change: a leader's perspective', in Henley Business School Graduate Student Paper (2012). Available at: https://henley.academia.edu/RodWillis

PART TWO
Case studies: learning culture in action

Lubricating learning: a case study of the WD-40 Company

05

Introduction

WD-40 is an extraordinary company. It is known for one single product, unchanged for decades, which most people reading this chapter will have in their garage, workplace or house. The company has expanded its range around that single product and has bought compatible brands, but it has not really changed its philosophy or approach. In spite of this, or perhaps because of this, the company is spectacularly successful and markets its products in 175 countries worldwide, and now manufactures in 25 locations around the world.

When the current CEO took over the company in 1997, it was a low-growth, profitable but unspectacular, limited market company that was cruising. He completely transformed the company by extending into a large number of new markets, acquiring a number of other household brands such as 3-in-One Oil, and consolidating the ubiquity of the product in the blue and yellow can.

This single product has been systematically extended into a range of WD-40 badged products from bikes to bulk industrial lubricants. The bottom line is that under the leadership of the current CEO, Garry Ridge, the market cap of the company over his 20-year journey has increased from $250 million to $1.9 billion. He joined the company 10 years previously, as the head of what was then a new regional office in Australia, covering Asia and the Pacific.

This case study will chart the extraordinary journey from that modest position in 1997, to the one that it currently occupies. The success of WD-40 is indelibly associated with an approach and philosophy, driven through the company, by the current Chief Executive. His firm belief in learning and the power of a learning organization to create the right environment for expansion and increased profitability has stood the test of time and stands as a beacon for others to follow. In a 2016 *Harvard Business Review* article by Bill Taylor he refers to the company as 'a learning obsessed company culture'. The article charts the development of the WD-40 Company under Ridge's leadership (Taylor, 2016a).

Ridge deliberately built the company around a culture of exploration, curiosity and innovation across the entire supply chain, and firmly linked widespread sharing of learning inside the organization and strong partnerships of trust with suppliers, to corporate success.

In doing this he created his own unique vocabulary to describe the organization. The employees are members of 'the tribe'. They say 'One world, One company, One tribe', but there are many 'tribal leaders'. The individual employee is a tribe member and his or her manager is known as a coach. The executive team is the Tribal Council who primarily uphold the tribal culture.

Ridge tabulates this as a series of tribal attributes (Figure 5.1).

On the one hand there are the four key attributes: living the values; a strong sense of belonging (like any tribe); a focus on moving forward and building and assuring the company's future; and finally a strong climate throughout the company of learning alongside the opportunity for teaching. It is that combination of strong values and constant learning, alongside a coaching/teaching ethos that defines the essential difference between the WD-40 Company and most other organizations. The Learning Moment, which owns the rights to the graphic below, is a separate organization, independent of the WD-40 Company, established by Garry Ridge to promote his vision of leadership and spread his concept of a learning organization. It offers tools and resources as well as consultancy to promote the development of learning organizations. Many hundreds of companies have taken the opportunity to learn from Garry's insights, based not on theory, but clear evidence of what happens in practice.

Figure 5.1   Tribal attributes

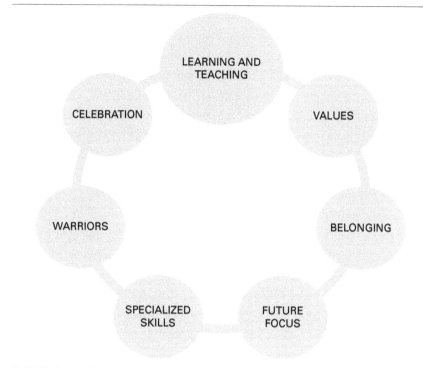

SOURCE The Learning Moment Inc. © 2017

The proof that something very special is going on in the WD-40 Company is brought into relief by the results of their employee engagement survey. This is conducted every two years and the 2018 figures are used here. Overall employee engagement stands at 93.3 per cent. Respect for my manager (referred to in the company as 'my coach') is at 96.4 per cent. 'I feel my opinions and values are a good fit with the WD-40 Company culture' is agreed by an astonishing 98.1 per cent of respondents. 'I love to tell people I work for WD-40 Company' was confirmed by 99 per cent of respondents. These figures are off the charts when compared to other engagement surveys. In 2016 the company identified the opportunity to increase global collaboration and set a path to do that. The company increased the employee score around collaboration from 74.2 per cent in 2016 to 84.7 per cent in 2018. This is a hugely significant increase in two years and a significant achievement.

The Gallup analysis of the state of the US workforce is a regular survey conducted since 2000, covering over one million workers (www.gallup.com/reports/199961/state-american-workplace-report-2017.aspx). The consistent headline, which hardly varies year to year, is that the average US company has around 33 per cent of its workforce who would describe themselves as 'engaged'. Exceptional companies, in Gallup's view, deliver 70 per cent engagement and reap the rewards of higher productivity (17 per cent), lower absenteeism (41 per cent), and lower attrition (24–59 per cent) as a result. These overall figures have hardly changed since 2000 when Gallup reported that 26 per cent of the workforce described themselves as engaged and 18 per cent described themselves as actively disengaged. The contrast with the WD-40 figures is stark. It is clear that the WD-40 Company is an exceptional operation. Ridge claims that the increase in employee engagement (in the high 30s when he took over, to 93 per cent today) mirrors and tracks the growth and success of the company by other metrics such as growth and profitability.

The Chairman and CEO of Gallup, Jim Clifton, comments in the Foreword to the 2017 Employee Engagement Survey Results publication:

> The American workforce has more than 100 million full-time employees. One-third of those employees are what Gallup calls engaged at work. They love their jobs and make their organization and make America better every day. At the other end, 16% of employees are actively disengaged – they are miserable in the workplace and destroy what the most engaged employees build. The remaining 51% of employees are not engaged – they're just there.

The strong overall engagement scores from the WD-40 Company hinge on two other measurements from their own Employee Engagement Survey. The first is about autonomy: 'I have the freedom to decide how to accomplish my objectives.' That statement is agreed by 90.6 per cent of staff. And secondly about respect and belonging: 94.5 per cent of staff agree that they are a valued member of their functional team. We need to dig down into the roots of this to track the relationship with learning.

There appears to be a remarkable contrast between the average employer and the WD-40 Company. This makes it a useful challenger company for this book, and offers some insights concerning the development of a learning culture and the building of a learning organization, as well as the relationship between learning and increased productivity as well as profitability.

Learning and values

Learning is endemic in the organization. The company focuses on extracting the learning from the process of strategy execution and makes this a continuous process and a keystone of the company culture. In other words, learning is an explicit contributor to the culture of the company. Ridge claims that 'the currency of power in WD-40 Company is knowledge' (personal communication, 5 May 2017). And this has broken down many of the corporate silos. Knowledge is gained by looking closely at what did not go to plan and turning these failures into 'learning moments'. They are sought out and the learning is extracted from them. A common question when staff meet is: 'What did you learn today?'

It is clear that this company does not focus on the negative elements of a mistake or failure but turns these elements into learning moments that are discussed and widely and rapidly disseminated around the organization. A learning moment is defined by the company as 'a positive or negative outcome of any situation that is shared openly to benefit all'. Anything that went better or worse than planned is 'a learning moment' and once the learning has been extracted, it is shared around the relevant teams. Every day is a learning challenge, and this links to fulfilment and motivation. And every day staff are encouraged to reflect on what they have learned and what they will, as a consequence, need to do differently for a negative outcome, or more of for a positive outcome.

In addition, the review system focuses solely on the values. The question between team member and coach/manager is, 'How have you lived the values?' And living the values is at the core of the organization, and is seen as the pathway to individual, team and corporate success. The values are 'not on the wall but engraved in our hearts', says Ridge (personal communication, May 2017). The collective view is that if the values are adhered to, the team member can work out what he or she needs to do with little guidance from a manager. When things go wrong, it is a values issue, not a failure to tick an objectives box, and it is also an opportunity to reflect and learn.

There is no need to probe deeply into how teams are formed; in many ways they are replicated in many similar manufacturing organizations. The issue is how they operate day to day. There is a culture of accountability and responsibility matched with candour and care. Staff are encouraged to deliver their objectives in whichever way they choose, but they still have to deliver their objectives. In Ridge's book, which he wrote with Ken Blanchard, he claims as 'simple truth 2' that 'helping people perform well' is about 'effective performance management systems' (Blanchard and Ridge, 2009: 94). It has three parts in the WD-40 Company. The first part is to set clear targets and performance standards. The second part is effective day-to-day coaching, which is about regularly praising progress and 'redirecting where necessary'. It is all about giving direction and support to help the employee succeed, and then success is shared in the review process, which is the third stage of performance management: performance evaluation.

The WD-40 Company calls this process 'review and learning' (Blanchard and Ridge, 2009: 95). The main review document, 'Goal Review Form' (Blanchard and Ridge, 2009: 194), divides staff into A+, A, B, L and C, and this is an amalgam of target meeting or exceeding, alongside living the six core values of the company. For example, to attain an A+ means setting a standard for others to follow and 'I consistently go above and beyond to demonstrate each corporate value, and I teach others how to demonstrate corporate values'. The 'L' category is 'Learning mode'. This is for new recruits or newly promoted staff. The indicators are, 'in the absence of my coach I cannot function independently' and 'I attempt to demonstrate corporate values, but I am not yet fully competent' (Blanchard and Ridge, 2009: 195). The corporate values are part of the review process, ie how each one is lived and what the behavioural indicators are for this. There is an overall quarterly rating for living the values that is graded in the same way as the targets are graded.

The values are not bland admonishments but core attributes for excellent performance. There are only six:

1 We value doing the right thing (Purpose).

2 We value creating positive lasting memories in all our relationships (Relationships).

3 We value making it better than it is today (Creative Innovation).

4 We value succeeding as a tribe while excelling as individuals (Trust and Teamwork).

5 We value owning it and passionately acting on it (Action).

6 We value sustaining the WD-40 Company economy (Economic Value).

The values are order ranked. This means that the first value dominates and guides an initial reaction, then the other values come into play one by one. Ridge claims the values are 'simple yet strong', 'they need to be clearly communicated as the only acceptable behaviour' (Blanchard and Ridge, 2009: 200). So, therefore, living the values is a profound discussion that can last many hours, and creates opportunities for coaching and support. The company feels that anything that goes wrong can be tracked back to the misalignment of the individual to the values, or a misinterpretation of the values. And there is no blame attached, only the opportunity to learn. But a continuing failure to learn is terminal. The lowest ranking in the review process is a 'C' and this is 'lack of effort' and 'little attempt to demonstrate corporate values'. Success, adhering to the values, and learning are all fundamentally linked.

The learning culture

The focus is on sharing not telling and building pride in the company as well as individual achievement. And coaches/managers are taught how to have coaching conversations that drive the required changes in behaviour. The company has a technical information repository called Blue Vault, which has been built up by staff and to which everyone has access when they need to know about any aspect of the company's processes, so that there is a conscious effort to ensure that people feel motivated to share their knowledge. The company wants all staff to feel that they belong, and there are regular ceremonies and celebrations in order to ensure that achievements are recognized.

Each staff member is given demanding stretch challenges to keep the company moving forward. For example, the turnover has doubled over the last 10 years and in Asia Pacific, the 2025 goal is to double the size of the market again. These goals are demanding and require resilience as well as innovation to achieve them. They are also long-term goals. The company refuses to publish quarterly returns and wants to be judged on the long-term trends rather than short-term expediency. Ridge refers to the 'vision-crushing ritual of quarterly earnings' and prefers to see profits as 'the applause for doing good work' (2017). The focus is on systematically building the company rather than posting increases in profit by any means necessary. Staff have a sense of themselves as warriors, fighting fierce battles while protecting each other and belonging to a strong and successful tribe.

Alongside this is a commitment by staff to move their own learning forward. Curiosity is cultivated, as is the habit of asking questions. This process of taking ownership and being empowered is enshrined in what Ridge calls the 'Maniac Pledge' that all staff are required to sign. The pledge simply states:

> I am responsible for taking action, asking questions, getting answers, and making decisions. I won't wait for someone to tell me. If I need to know, I am responsible for asking. I have no right to be offended that I did not get this sooner. If I am doing something others should know about, I am responsible for telling them.

That is a statement that enshrines the idea of 'permission to act'. Every staff member is explicitly empowered to share and ask when they do not know or understand. It is also a clear allocation of responsibility back to the individual, as well as an empowering statement for ownership and action. Constant learning and open discussion lubricate (pun intended) the entire organization.

But this churn of informal and social learning activity is coupled with more formal learning opportunities, particularly around leadership development. Currently, for example, 24 staff are being sponsored to complete the Master's in leadership at the University of San Diego (the location of the WD-40 Company's head office). There are leadership labs run by the company that have a specific syllabus and from which staff graduate. The main process of learning on these programmes is not a string of lectures but interaction and discussion around specific leadership ideas and behaviours.

The company tries hard to develop the concept of honesty and authenticity in their coaches/managers, which percolates down through the company as a whole. One explicit role for the coaches is to make any staff member's day meaningful and productive by offering support and by attempting to increase the positive and reduce any negative experiences. There is also a strong behavioural challenge. Coaches do not speak about any member of the company without imagining that the person in question, who is being talked about, is also in the same room. In other words, the company demands straight talking and tries hard to avoid hypocrisy and deceit. The company offers and demands clarity of purpose, honesty and a strong trust environment. There is no lying, no faking and no hiding.

By focusing on reducing staff stress, and increasing their quality of life, the company actually removes many barriers to optimum performance. The explicit aim of any tribe member's coach is to help that individual flourish and take away the inhibitors. The aim is to help that individual take charge of his or her own learning and empower that person to succeed.

The 'why' and the 'how' of the WD-40 Company defines an explicit role for each staff member. For example, the company's stated mission – the why the company exists – is 'to create positive lasting memories in everything we do. We solve problems. We make things work smoothly. We create opportunities.' If you substitute an 'I' for the 'We' in this statement, a purpose and a direction for everyone is obvious.

And 'how' that mission is delivered draws explicitly on the role of learning: 'We create positive lasting memories by the cultivation of learning and teaching which produces a highly engaged workforce who live our company's values every day.'

The 'what' of the WD-40 Company is about the products. The company 'deliver unique, high value and easy-to-use solutions for a wide variety of maintenance needs in workshops, factories and homes. We market and distribute our brands across multiple trade channels in countries all over the world.' And it rewards achievement.

Bonuses are awarded on a combination of country, regional and global targets. And bonuses are triggered the moment the performance equals or exceeds 5 per cent above target. This is an annual payment, and last year the bonus pot was over $15 million (among 450 staff), which represented between 15 and 19 per cent of each staff member's remuneration.

The company also excels in terms of its relationships with its customers. There is no other lubricant company that has a fan club, for example. A corner of its website focuses on selling and illustrating collectable cans, and there is a place for customers to upload their stories about how they use the product. Buying just one can of WD-40 almost gives you an entry ticket into an enthusiasts' club!

In other words, Ridge tries to imbue the company with a high-level purpose that resonates and defines how staff and suppliers relate to the company. This encompasses what staff should do, how they should behave and how success is defined as well as the kind of status and relationship with outside suppliers, distributors and manufacturers.

The company consciously tries to generate stories and life moments relating to their products rather than just talk about cans of lubricant. The WD-40 Company helps millions of people all over the world smooth out life's wrinkles! If that sounds over the top, read the stories of dire circumstances averted by the use of the product that are celebrated on the company website (www.wd40.com). The company lists 1,000 uses for the product under the guise, 'Did you know...?' The website contains hundreds of short video clips (as short as eight seconds) demonstrating these benefits of the product and gathered under three macro headings of 'home, work and play'. All of this under the tag line: 'Live life hands on. Explore solutions.' If the company referred to itself as simply a lubricant manufacturer, it would not have a fraction of the same resonance. In fact, Ridge describes his company's products as 'problem solvers and memory creators', ridding the world of 'squeaks, smells, and dirt' (Taylor WD-40 case study, 2016).

Ridge also uses the history of the company to positive effect. The company was originally Rocket WD-40, linked to a product developed for the US space programme in the 1950s. The spray was specifically developed as a water displacement chemical for NASA rockets, rather than as a lubricant. As Ridge proudly tells people, the WD stands for water displacement and the number '40' is because it was only when they developed the 40th formulation that it finally did the job. Never has the statement 'it does what it says on the tin' been more accurate than in the case of WD-40.

What is the company like to work for?

Garry Ridge is an Australian. He discusses regularly how he has been influenced by aboriginal culture in terms of the language he uses, and the way he has structured the WD-40 Company. For example, the senior executive group are referred to as the Tribal Council. He talks explicitly about building a tribal culture; his staff are encouraged to see themselves as warriors, and their leaders as elders and teachers with a Global Leadership Council to oversee the work of the company as a whole. Glassdoor, which is the website where employees and former employees are encouraged to post anonymous (and therefore more honest) accounts of their current or former employer has a number of WD-40 Company postings. They overwhelmingly back the account that the CEO has shared in this chapter. They draw attention to the values-driven culture and the passion of the people who work for the company and how long staff remain with what is, after all, a small company. One describes it as 'one big family and that is not something you get everywhere'. There is appreciation for the learning opportunities offered, the chance to travel and the decent health and pension benefits.

But not everything is perfect. The comments are overwhelmingly positive but there are some cons. There is criticism of the poor collaboration across global sites (something Ridge has tackled recently) and resource constraints.

Each Glassdoor review ends with advice to the company management that is, again, extremely positive, mostly asking the company to keep up the good work and acknowledging the caring management, which one person said was very refreshing for corporate America. There are 33 reviews from employees or ex-employees of the company. The overall rating is 4.2/5.0, and the CEO Garry Ridge receives a 100 per cent approval rating. These figures are very hard to match. Google, a renowned and desirable employer, achieves a 4.4 rating and the CEO Sundar Pichai has a 96 per cent approval rating. A small and well-liked company such as Logitech (therefore a more realistic comparison) achieves a 3.9 rating, and the CEO Bracken Darrell gets a 97 per cent approval rating.

The leadership approach

The leadership philosophy and approach has been developed over the 20 years of Garry Ridge's CEO tenure. He began with two or three core philosophies that have stood the test of time. He did not want micro-management in his company, and he has an enduring belief in the power of the leader as an enabler and coach. He also believed that leaders needed to be developed and they should be given the right tools in order to be effective. These beliefs endure to this day.

The role of a WD-40 Company leader is, simply, to get the best from the staff that they manage. If the leaders serve their people, their people will serve their customers, and the company will flourish. It is a simple philosophy that has been elaborated and codified over the years but in essence has remained consistent. Ridge is quoted in a Ken Blanchard Company case study summing up this philosophy and approach as:

> Having a clear purpose, a set of values that provide a safe working environment, and a common language of leadership makes learning moments something to cherish – not something to fear. Some of our most powerful learnings come from negative situations. Our tribe members understand the importance of sharing information for the greater good. (https://resources.kenblanchard.com/client-spotlights/wd-40-company)

At the core of this approach is trust. Without that, mistakes would never be admitted to, and knowledge would not be shared. And trust depends on developing a safe workplace environment where people actually care about the well-being of staff. This phrase 'leaders actually care' comes from one of the Glassdoor reviews (www.glassdoor.com). Ridge again: 'We expect tribal leaders to care about their people, to be candid with them, to hold them accountable and responsible. In order to do that, tribe leaders and tribe members have to work together to set goals and define what good performance looks like' (https://resources.kenblanchard.com/client-spotlights/wd-40-company).

The culture is open, challengeable and based around trust and autonomy for the individual, but within a clear frame of understanding what is required to do the job. Expectations, of both the leader and the team member, are clarified, codified and shared. The implications of this are clearly reflected in the company's healthy and engaging working environment where people try to help, are genuinely friendly and happy to share the knowledge freely with each other. A direct by-product of this is longevity of employment inside the company; the downside may be a lack of innovation, which the organization attempts to compensate for by learning and sharing.

The website shares a vast number of clever ideas that have extended the reach and popularity of the products. The emphasis on constant learning and sharing of new knowledge clearly has had a dramatic impact on the ability of the company to renew itself on a regular basis. In spite of the company having a comfortable and attractive culture, and consistent sales in all it markets, it is neither arrogant nor complacent. There is a range of products that reflect changing lifestyles, and a club-membership philosophy based on encouraging customers to celebrate their success with the product and share new uses that they have discovered. The company, in its turn, offers hints and tips about extending the value of the product in different environments.

How to build a learning organization: lessons from the WD-40 Company

There are at least seven lessons that emerge from looking at the WD-40 Company that can be applied generally to other organizations wanting to use learning as a driver for performance.

1 A learning organization starts from the top

Garry Ridge is a critical part of the success of the company. Clearly the values and approach that he exemplifies run strongly and consistently through the company. As CEO he built the company with a clear vision of the way he wanted it to operate. Since his tenure as CEO of the company, over 20 years so far, he has consolidated his position, and its growth and success have reinforced that approach. The proof that this approach works is in the growth and profitability of the company. He has not changed his core beliefs, and in some ways he has become more, rather than less, committed to them over the years.

The fact that his empowerment-based and learning-led philosophy is working well has encouraged him to share that vision with an increasing number of people beyond his company, and partner with well-established management gurus such as Ken Blanchard (famous for his 'One Minute Manager' series of books and setting up the Blanchard Group of Companies that deliver Blanchard's philosophy into other companies) and coach Marshall Goldsmith (often called the 'world's most famous coach', he works with CEOs from Fortune 500 companies and has written widely about business behaviours that lead to success), with whom he shares similar values. He has therefore become an advocate for the benefits that accrue to those brave enough to commit to building high staff engagement, learning organizations.

Ridge is by far the company's best-known employee, and owns the culture and vision going forward. And he is increasingly developing a high profile outside the business. He recently joined Marshall Goldsmith's 100 coaches 'pay it forward' programme. This, by invitation, group of elite coaches, business leaders and academics, is an esteemed group who will continue to be mentored and developed by Marshall Goldsmith, for no cost provided. They, in their turn, share their expertise with others in a similar way. So that initial 100 members of the group that work with Goldsmith, could potentially nurture over 10,000 others as a direct consequence. Ridge is still only one of 16 business leaders across the United States to make the Goldsmith cut. The others represent far bigger organizations. It is clear that Ridge and his philosophy have traction and credibility.

2 Trust is the momentum and energy for a learning organization

It is hard to imagine how any kind of learning organization could flourish in the absence of trust. The reach of trust is extensive in the company. It lies at the core of the behaviour expected of tribal members and their leaders. Trust helps develop a culture of openness internally and helps the company do business much quicker externally.

I have isolated at least six elements of trust inside the company. The first is about full disclosure; the company publishes its sales, income and investment figures for staff as a matter of course. There is open discussion about strategy and performance. The second is related to the first. There are no secrets about salaries or bonus levels. Everybody is aware of what everybody else is paid throughout the company. This means there are no hidden deals or obvious injustices around salary levels. It is also true, according to Glassdoor reviews, that salaries are not especially high in the company but are considered fair and open to scrutiny (www.glassdoor.com.au/Reviews/WD-40-Company-Reviews-E2021.htm).

Thirdly, all staff are expected to admit mistakes. Everything that is judged unsuccessful is scrutinized and the learning extracted so that it can guide and inform future actions. In other words, there is a very strong cultural push to eliminate any covering up or blaming others for poor performance. No one feels threatened or feels the need to escape the consequences of dealing with things that did not work. There is almost a culture of celebrating failure in order that the learning can be extracted rapidly and circulated around the organization. No one is punished for admitting something has gone wrong. However, anyone not learning from mistakes and consistently making the same mistake again and again is asked to leave the company. A learning organization means what it says.

The fourth element of trust is a profound cultural imperative for staff to help one another. No one is intentionally left struggling. Everyone is encouraged to ask for help. Problems are solved by pooling insight and knowledge. The fifth trust element is the relationship between staff and manager/coach. Discussions are forthright and honest. Managers are encouraged to trust their direct reports, and staff are encouraged to share what is actually going in their work with their coach, and be candid in terms of their progress in meeting their objectives.

The final element is the shared belief that the company tries to do good in the world and behave in an ethical manner at all times with staff, suppliers and customers. That leads directly to the pride staff demonstrate in working for the company, as cited above.

3 A learning organization needs time to take root and flourish

The timeframes in the WD-40 Company are more extended than in many organizations. This company is not driven by quarterly growth and profit targets. It is staff growth and learning value that is reviewed on a quarterly basis! Longevity is a central part of the company culture, so initiatives are able, for the most part, to take their own time. And targets can be long term, such as the one to double the size of WD-40 Company presence in Asia by 2025. The board backs the CEO and accepts his timescales, even if the return on investment is extended as a result. The key is that the growth is reliable and consistent over time, not erratic and irregular.

This is also true of the staff. The company does not recruit on the basis that most new employees will be gone within two years. The longevity of WD-40's employees, despite it being a relatively small organization employing only 450 staff worldwide, is quite remarkable. Ridge's 20 years at the top are matched by many other employees throughout the organization. Staff stay because they like the place and because they respect the company's mission.

4 Leadership is cherished

The company invests a remarkable amount of money into building good leadership throughout the organization. It sponsors relatively large numbers of staff to acquire Masters' qualifications at the University of San Diego (where Ridge is an adjunct Professor himself) and it has an integrated, internal leadership programme for all those in leadership positions. The leadership philosophy is based on a coaching model that is enshrined in the business philosophy that Garry Ridge conceived and wrote up in his book with Ken Blanchard (2009). The philosophy is called 'Don't mark my paper, help me get an A' and the book is called *Helping People Win at Work*. It is part of more extended partnership between Garry Ridge and the Ken Blanchard group of companies. The WD-40 Company has one of the standard case studies used by the group in its own leadership development programmes.

The book outlines the overall leadership philosophy that is espoused by Blanchard and Ridge, which can be summed up in two words: candour and caring. It is based around a coaching model designed to help staff achieve their best. This is based on the belief that the biggest impact on performance comes from day-to-day coaching. This coaching experience should accentuate the positive and help staff learn and build on their mistakes. The company demands high-quality leadership and refers to its leaders as 'coaches' to emphasize the primacy of that approach. This term is preferred to 'manager' or 'leader'. Everyone expects support, honesty and rigorous performance management, but also the chance to improve, to learn more, and progress through the company. This is part of delivering an empowered workforce. As has been stated elsewhere in this book, an empowered workforce is a critical building block for a learning organization.

5 Learning organizations are values driven

The WD-40 Company is clearly a values-driven organization. The company has six core values, which are described on page 129. Garry Ridge describes that the values as the fundamental building blocks for the culture of the company (personal communication, May 2017). He decries organizations that frame their values and mount them on the wall in the reception area but they mean nothing to staff and do not determine any behaviour. The WD-40 Company tries to live the values, without exception, at all times and discussion about them forms the core of the review process.

The values are a staple of the coaching sessions that support and develop an individual in the company. It is impossible to succeed in the company without using the values as a benchmark for behaviour and a guideline for action. Explaining and elaborating the values forms a key element of the induction process, and they are presented as living statements about how you should behave, rather than synthetic constructs without depth or meaning.

They cover all aspects of the company, from developing economic value to creative innovation. They describe individual as well as teamwork excellence, but there is a deliberate absence of the word 'learning'. The reason for this is that a learning organization imbues learning across the whole spectrum of activities and behaviours; it is not separate or isolated. Learning emerges out of each of the values, rather than being a separate value in itself.

The values are laid out in a hierarchy of priority so that the first, 'We value doing the right thing', sets the standard and the context for the other values. And doing the right thing is a broad-brush statement that describes correct behaviour in terms of one's colleagues, direct reports, customers, suppliers and manufacturers.

6 Learning organizations have a clear focus on innovation, value creation and doing the right thing

The WD-40 Company has an extremely rigorous focus on its growth, profitability and success. There is an obsession in the WD-40 Company with ensuring insights are shared. Staff are routinely asked, 'what did you learn today?' And information is constantly added to their knowledge repository, as well as shared through company blogs and social media. This is the same for teams working in every location, and staff are encouraged to share and to learn across the entire company. There is no sense that the organization distracts itself from the fundamental object of its existence: profitably building products and services that make a difference.

The regular performance reviews focus on delivery of objectives, which mostly relate to the development of the business. That unrelenting focus on building and developing the company is a strong characteristic of the organization. And the organization encourages a strong element of curiosity in staff. They are encouraged to challenge the status quo, and come up with better products, or better delivery to market of those products. This builds a workforce that is focused and resilient. Everyone has a clear mandate, is conscious of the role they play and is aware about what constitutes success. Every assistance is given to help them succeed. Nothing is allowed to detract from that focus on action and delivery.

7 Reward needs to be transparent and fair

The company's reward model is based on a combination of individual, team, region and overall company performance. The maximum rewards are only given out at times when the company, as a whole, does exceptionally well; the region in which an individual works is achieving its objectives, and that person's team is doing a good job. And then the individual comes into the equation. The company recognized from the very beginning that simply rewarding individual achievement is not sufficient.

The reward system is also designed to reinforce the sharing ethos. Therefore the entire company expects all individuals to generate new insights and knowledge and share those around the organization as fast as possible. If people feel good about themselves they will perform; if they perform, the company as a whole will benefit; if the company benefits then the staff will be rewarded. There is a huge incentive to make the company successful, and to help ensure their success by coaching, and by supporting. This is critical part of the simple success formula.

Conclusions

It is easy to dismiss the WD-40 Company as a one-of-its-kind organization. It has unique features, this is true. For example, very few other companies have a single product that has endured for so long and could be indispensable for decades to come. And of course, few organizations have a CEO as charismatic and driven as Garry Ridge. But none of this explains the continuing growth and success of the company. The product does not sell itself, and a CEO cannot be responsible for everything that happens inside the company. There is clearly something else going on that is replicable. Copying the WD-40 Company would be naïve and counter-productive. But there are a number of core elements that define the way the company operates, which have genuine applicability and resonance across any number of organizations.

At the heart of the company's success is learning. Staff are challenged to grow, expand their knowledge beyond the simple prescribed objectives, and be curious. But this quest for insight is not delivered in a woolly and vague way. The WD-40 Company has a number of simple rules and values that are not optional. One of the driving forces in the company is to seek clarity. Everybody is expected to know what they need to achieve, and to what standard. Staff are encouraged to use their initiative to work through and resolve any ambiguity. The manager/coach has a role, almost exclusively built around helping and supporting direct reports. A manager/coach's job is to encourage that member of staff to grow, learn and become a better and more valuable contributor as each year passes. Every single employee is made to feel valued and a significant member of their team as well as of the company overall. The day-to-day business of the company is conducted in an atmosphere of candour and openness. There should be no surprises, no hidden agendas or discussion behind anyone's back. What you need to hear you will hear directly. In addition, staff are expected to work hard and their success is rewarded. This is not a complicated formula.

The company has a whole series of alignments at its heart. The growth and success of the individual should relate directly to the growth and success of the company. The company's values determine how people should behave. The behaviour of all staff should lead to a coherent and benevolent culture that focuses on learning and growth. Each individual should have stretch targets that align to the stretch targets the organization sets itself going forward. An appropriate timescale is allocated for the achievement of those targets at both individual and organizational level. Teams are at the heart of the company and individuals are expected to always have team success in mind, alongside individual achievement. At the same time, a team should always have the overall success of the organization in mind.

The learning element is designed to offer challenge but also membership of a great club that has a lot of fun. Any detailed analysis of company's website will reveal a conscious attempt to create a club. This is one part practical and one part whimsical. The company seeks out the unusual, the eccentric and the one-off, while emphasizing the intensely practical nature of the products that the company produces.

The company manages to convince us that a can of lubricant really does make our life better. The same can builds a mission and purpose for staff to rally around. All of this relates directly to learning. Just as the customer learns new uses for the product, the member of staff learns how best to put more product in more hands and in more places.

The overwhelming conclusion is that if you can build an organization full of engaged, motivated staff, whose thirst for new knowledge is encouraged, anything is possible. This company shows the value of continuous learning, based around shared insight and a laser-like focus on achieving objectives. There is nothing magical about the success of the WD-40 Company. It is a clear demonstration that a strong learning culture wrapped inside a learning company actually delivers. This creates a great place to work that is not 'great' at the expense of profitability and success, but a direct product of that success. The WD-40 Company builds passionate, purpose-driven people, guided by values, who deliver amazing outcomes.

References

Blanchard, K and Ridge, G (2009) *Helping People Win at Work*, Pearson Education Inc, New Jersey

Ridge, G (July 2017) Podcast on Leadership: http://yscouts.com/interviews/garry-ridge-podcast-ceo-of-wd40/

Taylor, B (2016a) How WD-40 created a learning-obsessed company culture, *Harvard Business Review*, 16 September

Taylor, B (2016) *Simply Brilliant*, Penguin Books

Happy Ltd and HT2: learning culture in action

06

The background to Happy Ltd

Over 30 years ago, in 1987, life did not appear so wonderful for Henry Stewart, the founder and Chief Happiness Officer of Happy Ltd. He had joined a small team that had raised £6.5 million in order to establish a brand new, radical Sunday newspaper, *The News on Sunday* (*Guardian*, 2016). Henry played many roles, ending up as Finance Manager. He watched helplessly as the internal squabbling led to a chronic inability to make decisions or build strategy and stick to it. One memorable low point was when the leadership team agreed to a poster campaign and spent £85,000 on getting thousands printed before changing their mind, deciding not to use them, and then scrapping the whole lot. This created not just an enormously unpleasant and dysfunctional working environment, but a hugely loss-making one as well.

The brilliant, ambitious and challenging endeavour crashed and burned. Within six weeks the money was gone and the newspaper declared bankruptcy. Though it got funding to stagger on for a few more months, 200 people were to lose their jobs. Henry had watched it happen without being able to stop it. It was a life-changing experience. As a direct result of that business disaster, Henry decided to set up his own company and run it in a completely different way. That was the origin of Happy Ltd. And it was designed from the outset to be the exact opposite of the workplace that had nearly destroyed him: principled, efficient and, above all, a great place to work.

He decided to offer a different kind of training in basic software and project management skills that would take away the fear many people felt when confronted with new software packages and create learners who wanted to learn and had fun learning. And he wanted a workplace that embodied those values of openness, transparency and personal growth. He called the company Happy Computers. It was established, claimed Henry, 'both to make learning about IT an enjoyable experience, and to discover how to make a truly great place to work' (www.happy.co.uk/about-happy/founders/).

Thirty years on, there are now three companies operating under the banner of Happy Ltd. And the company is doing very well. If you call your company Happy Ltd you are setting a high bar! But the results fully justify the name; it was voted the best company in the UK for customer service, and one of the top 20 best workplaces for five successive years. So impressive was the culture and approach to work that – in response to demand – the company set up a division in 2003 called Happy People to show others how to increase engagement at work. Later it partnered with LVSC to offer soft skills training for the voluntary sector.

Henry was included in the 2011 Guru Radar section of the Thinkers50 list of the up-and-coming thinkers with important ideas. 'He is one of the thinkers who we believe will shape the future of business', explained the list compiler Stuart Crainer.

The happy ethos

For Henry, trust is the conscious core of the culture and the aim is for the company to demonstrate that at every turn. There is an openness among all staff, together with a sense that you could ask the same question and get exactly the same answer regardless of who was responding, and what level they worked at in the company. Henry has a phrase that he uses all the time: 'Do not believe me, ask my staff.' And as we saw from Chapter 5, trust is the absolute centre of any learning culture.

Learning, and the willingness and ability to learn, are at the heart of the recruitment process in the company. Potential employees are asked to learn about a new software package as part of the interview process, and then teach others to use it. And in order to test their flexibility and resilience, the 15 minutes of presentation time that they were told they had, is abruptly changed! The company recruits staff who are not phased by this rapid change of plan, and revel in the challenge presented. Working for Happy offers opportunities to learn fast. This goes hand in hand with the chance to be stretched and challenged. In spite of Happy being a small company, there are carefully crafted opportunities for staff to develop their career, whether it is into leadership roles or more technically specialist roles. People are encouraged to move around, and there is an active process that helps people discover what they are good at, alongside a culture that encourages staff to become curious and lifelong learners.

The company celebrates a culture of openness. This means that, wherever possible, everything is shared, and little happens behind closed doors. There is a clear policy that no one is fed to the lions when they make a mistake, and everyone is encouraged to admit what they do not know and to own up when things go wrong. These basic principles are the key to sustaining innovation as far as Stewart is concerned.

The key elements of the Happy culture are so strong and obvious that Henry Stewart decided to write them down. They were published in a book called the *Happy Manifesto* in 2012. There are 10 elements listed and the book outlines how they emerged, and how anyone else could implement them. The book acts as both Henry Stewart's and the company's calling card and thousands of copies have been distributed over the world. And although the book does not contain one separate element focused solely on lifelong learning, learning radiates through at least 7 of the 10 elements.

In the introduction to the book, the author asks the reader to:

Imagine a workplace where people are energised and motivated by being in control of the work they do. Imagine being trusted and given freedom, within clear guidelines, to decide how to achieve the results. Imagine they are able to get the life balance they want. Imagine they are valued according to the work they do, rather than the number of hours they spend at their desk. (Stewart, 2012)

He then asks whether anyone would like to work in such a place. The answer is obvious, and more than a pipe dream. The outcome can be achieved if you have a core philosophy based on an overriding belief that if you try to get the best out of everyone, you will achieve engagement and productivity as a result.

The company works on the principle that managers should get out of the way and let people work out what they need to do and offer support when asked. There is an anti-micromanagement ethos taken to a logical extreme where projects and innovations are 'pre-approved'. In other words, the team involved do not have to refer back once the project gets the green light. Staff are trusted to do the job, and expected to come up with their own solutions and implement them with no reference back if there are no problems. This puts the onus on individuals and their ability to learn rapidly.

In some organizations, these are called 'stretch assignments' and reserved for fast-track management to accelerate their development. In Happy Ltd it is the normal way of working for everyone. All staff are encouraged to take ownership and make small changes, regardless of where they work in the organization. As an example, the receptionist was given a small budget to improve the look and feel of reception once she understood the culture and the aspirations of Happy. She did not need to get approval for what she spent. It was her domain.

You could argue that this is a relatively small concession, but the company also pre-approved one member of staff to completely redesign the company website. The first time Stewart saw the new website was when he logged on for the first time after it had been launched. This is a massive endorsement, and would have been an extraordinary, powerful learning opportunity for the individual concerned. Even Stewart admitted in the book that this was a scary thing to do (Stewart, 2012).

Rather like the WD-40 Company (see Chapter 5) and HT2, staff are coached rather more than managed. One of the precepts of the company is: 'do not tell when you can ask'. Everyone is encouraged to take responsibility, and this includes responsibility for running the staff meetings. Each staff meeting is run by different group of staff, and those in charge are free to choose how they do it. One team did it through song.

The company also attempts to match work life with the rest of your life. How you do your job should be how you run your life. And no one is expected to sacrifice the latter for the former. The core business is teaching others, and this is done through involving learners and telling great stories. The aim is to deliver a fantastic, memorable experience, not just a course. The outcomes have to be positive as well as productive. Exactly the same philosophy runs through the organization.

The company structure is fairly flat, and the basic structure of the organization is team-based. Each team does have a leader (normally selected by the team), whose job it is to have overall responsibility, attend the exec meeting on behalf of the team, develop and promote a better working environment and deliver successful outcomes. Separately every member of the team has a co-ordinator, whose role is to coach and support (and challenge) the person and help them so that they get better at what they do. The co-ordinator is chosen by the individual and may or may not be the leader of the team. Indeed, they may not even be part of that team. There are parallels here with the WD-40 Company (see Chapter 5).

Proof that this is working is not left to chance. Coupled with this approach is a no blame culture. Mistakes are celebrated and become learning opportunities, not punishment points, and the whole process is lubricated with learning. For example, there are trainers' days once per month where the 'each one, teach one' philosophy is applied. Staff are free to share their expertise and free to learn. Everyone is encouraged to do a bit of both. It helps the trainers perfect their teaching, share their knowledge and become effective and efficient learners. This overt and structured learning is coupled with permission to find time to learn whenever it is possible. In order to do this space has to be created in the working week and one of Henry Stewart's current aspirations is not to increase the workload for staff but to decrease it in order to create that space for reflection and learning. His belief is that this will actually improve the quality of the day-to-day work and make the company more productive and profitable not less.

Henry Stewart also proudly boasts about the times when staff deliberately challenged his views. They quietly worked on projects that he would not have approved of in the early stages if he had been asked to. He calls this 'innovation to the point of disobedience' (Stewart, 2012). The critical point is not the learning involved, rather the consequences of the learning. If staff are to be empowered they need to make decisions and be trusted to make the right decisions. If staff are going to innovate, they have to try new things in new ways. A by-product of innovation is always learning. No one can get by without having to find out new things. And that process starts right from the very first recruitment interview when potential staff are given a new piece of software to learn. But, as Stewart is quick to point out, this is freedom within guidelines. It is not what Stephen M R Covey in *The Speed of Trust* (2006) calls blind trust, but what he refers to as 'smart trust' (see Chapter 4). Henry Stewart defines this idea of freedom within guidelines as: 'trust 90%'! There is the need to reassure and lightly check when necessary.

Just as all staff working for the company are expected to be flexible, agile and adaptable to meet the needs of their customers, no less is expected of Happy Ltd. It has done exactly the same, when it pivoted in order to meet new, identifiable opportunities. These big shifts in focus would not have been remotely possible without the strong commitment of staff, their belief in their own learning, as well as their belief in the company as a whole and its future. For this reason, Henry Stewart describes the culture of the company as 'emerging, rather than fixed'.

Learning is not a nice to have aspect of the company culture, but is at the core of what it does and how it survives. And that willingness to listen and change viewpoint includes the CEO. Recently, some staff members walked Stewart through a new procedure. He agreed it was better than the old one and was happy to endorse the change based on their experience and their recommendation. Increasingly staff do not even ask, they just do it!

And any learning culture is predicated on sharing rather than hoarding experience, ideas, expertise and knowledge. The physical layout of an organization can either hinder this or support it. In Happy Ltd all the staff sit in the main, open-plan workroom, including Henry himself. This proximity allows easy sharing of ideas and asking for help. It is called 'The Hub' and it is the beating heart of the company. It backs onto a kitchen/reception area where free tea and coffee, and often food, are made available, with ice creams at 4 pm each afternoon for delegates and staff alike. The office ambience reflects the company. A hall alcove has been decorated to look like a train compartment, with two seats and a window that looks out onto a pleasant rural setting. The lights in the reception/coffee area look like multicoloured balloons stuck to the ceiling with their pull chords designed to look like string. It is impossible not to smile when you walk into the offices of Happy Ltd.

The core business is helping others learn and building better work-places. This is done in a way that involves the customer and is built around telling great stories. The aim is to ensure that all the participants, whatever their interaction with Happy Ltd, have a fantastic experience that is enduring as well as productive.

The company gathers feedback on everything every day, whenever a customer is involved, and whenever coordinators meet with their team. Proof that everything is working is not left to chance. There are Happy check surveys regularly. No one in the company is allowed to duck their personal responsibility to make things right. Everyone is expected to be vigilant, take note when things need to be fixed, and ensure that things get done.

Henry Stewart does not extract himself from any of these obligations or processes. He deliberately sets an example. He listens, takes feedback and he learns. His aim is to read 50 books a year, and to clear space in his calendar to do this. And he shares his insights. One personal productivity method he has implemented is the 321zero method of email management. This simply demands that individuals look at their email only three times a day, and complete that task within 21 minutes, reducing their inbox to zero each time. He also uses the 'eat four frogs a day' task-setting scheme. This means writing down at the end of each day four key tasks that you have to complete the next day. The aim is to complete at least one of them before you touch your email. This personal productivity rubs off on the whole Happy community.

What do the staff think?

These ideas and challenges are transparently shared with staff, and they are encouraged to find their own pathways to being more efficient and effective. No one is told what to do, no one is commanded to use particular models as long as they are within the company guidelines, but everyone focuses on making the company successful and ensuring their own contribution to that. In many ways, then, learning is the gyroscope for the organization. It keeps it steady and points to new directions, and can spot advancing turbulence but remain steady. This createsa sense of purpose and confidence. There is a pride in what has been achieved, and a sense that the organization can overcome difficulty and disruption. Everyone fundamentally believes in the capability of the company, and trusts in the competence and commitment of the workforce.

At a Happy staff meeting, staff were asked to share some of their thoughts around the company's learning culture. When asked how big a part learning played in terms of their engagement with the company, the answers were very strong:

> 'It's a huge part. I love to constantly learn new things and develop, and I'm in the perfect place for this.'
>
> 'I like that I'm encouraged to develop skills, and I have opportunities for training; for example, I always wanted to learn Photoshop, now I can!'
>
> 'I like that we are encouraged to learn, and we are given a budget to do it.'
>
> '[Learning] is part of everyone's development plan. It needs to be central. It underpins everything we do.'
>
> 'It is crucial. It is how we grow and innovate individually and as a business.'

And the learning methods are both formal and informal. Staff like that mixture: 'A lot of informal: twitter, blogs, videos. But also, quite a lot of conferences, workshops etc.'

When asked in what ways are you a better learner now than a few years ago, the replies revealed a growing maturity as learners: 'I put things in context of a much larger process or system now'; 'I try to action what I learned more immediately'; and 'I make time to do learning – before I wanted to, but was too busy.'

That culture of learning has big ramifications for the way work is done. For example, one member of staff volunteered that:

'Everyone is very helpful and happy to share tips. The open-plan office also helps. There is lots of on-the-job learning.'

'I have passed on good tips to others to help make their work easier.'

'People are often teaching each other practical skills to make their job easier.'

There is nothing special about learning in the Happy Company. It is neither put on a pedestal nor seen as something exceptional. It is the way things are done, and therefore it is strongly embedded in the culture. Every member of staff I talked to related and conflated their own learning journeys with the success and stability of the organization. Their motivation and the opportunities to learn and experiment were not in addition to day-to-day work, but had actually become embedded in the day-to-day work.

Ensuring everybody is up to speed in all key in areas of the business, and that productivity is increased by offering the widest possible support and regularly circulating tips and ideas, is felt to be no more than business as usual in Happy Ltd; in other words, the way work is done. If any small business has to be nimble, agile and willing to pivot, it needs staff who are willing to change and to think their way out of problems. The aim is to make the company more successful and more innovative than it was before. And there is a core belief that this is both desirable and possible. If there is a strange noise around the Happy Company office, it is the whirring of brains rather than sighs of indifference.

HT2 Labs: How enabling learning enables a learning organization

HT2 is a young Oxford-based tech company whose explicit aim is to 'make learning more personal, more social and more measurable'. The name stands for: high tech, high touch. It is an R&D company that builds products that emerge from its own research and takes an evidence-based approach to confirm the validity and functionality of its products.

The company has three core software offerings that it has developed and marketed as a package. The most recent is Red Panda. This is their personal learning hub, which enables learners to curate their own learning journeys and track their learning goals. Their most significant product is Curatr, a social learning platform for spreading knowledge and enabling community-based learning. Finally, they market Learning Locker, which is built on the open-source xAPI protocol that tracks learning and measures the extent and impact of learning on business performance: 'xAPI is an e-learning software specification that allows learning content and learning systems to speak to each other in a manner that records and tracks all types of learning experiences' (Wikipedia).

It is an extremely unusual tech company in one aspect of its existence: both the father, Alan Betts, and his son, Dr Ben Betts, work in the company. Indeed, it was founded by Alan Betts and he then ceded the Chief Executive role to Ben, while remaining in the company as its CLO.

Learning is core to the company for two crucial reasons. Firstly, it is part of their staff retention strategy. By allowing staff to develop and expand into roles that they are interested in, and by encouraging them to learn new skills, retention is exceptional. People stay because it is a great place to work. All of these new skills are brought back into the company to enhance its overall capability.

To illustrate this, one member of staff was recruited as a solutions architect, but rapidly invented an entirely new role of 'customer success manager' for himself. He works with large customers to smooth the implementation of HT2 products and help ensure their success. It is a powerful role that had not been available previously until the individual spotted the need and moved to meet it.

Another example is a member of staff who was recruited as a level 3 customer service apprentice. Within a month he moved on to a degree programme with the Open University and is now migrating into a data security role with the company. In fact, 25 per cent of staff are being supported as they tackle large formal qualifications. Two are working towards Doctorates, one is on a Master's course and one is studying for a first degree.

The second reason is that learning helps maintain the R&D focus of the company. If you can sustain curiosity and insight, you automatically build resilience. The resilience of the staff gives the company an edge, improves its alignment with customers and keeps the products fresh and relevant. The stability of the core team creates a sense of a big family and builds commitment. Given the cost of recruiting, and the subsequent loss of knowledge when people leave, HT2's policy of an active retention strategy is much more enlightened and useful. The company's investment of time and money encouraging people to stay handsomely pays off. The proof that this policy is working is evidenced by the fact that no one has left the company in the last two years. This is a remarkable achievement for a small company working in a sector where jobs and opportunities are plentiful.

This goes hand in hand with a strong approach to work/life balance. No one is required to work late or over the weekend. The belief is that people are exhausted by 4 pm on Friday, so the office winds down early, and everyone is allowed to socialize and have a bit of fun before going home. There is a conscious effort not to push anyone past their own natural productive limit. This keeps staff sharp and focused, and it keeps them loyal.

People are encouraged to work to their cognitive capacity; this means that they do not have to sit at their desk for a set number of hours. If a member of staff wants to go for a walk, they are encouraged to do that (and take one of the dogs). Productivity is not tracked in a crude way, eg expecting staff to deliver 120 lines of code every working day. The deeper issues are much more important: sometimes lots of code can be written quickly, and sometimes real problems have to be solved first. The company trusts that everyone will do their best.

What staff are asked to do, however, is work out loud. Everybody notes down in a common journal what they are going to achieve that day, what they achieved yesterday, and what are their blockers and what help they might need. All of this activity is aggregated three times a day, so that remote-working staff, as well as the US team, have a clear picture of what is going on across the whole company. They also use Slack as their main internal communications tool, and it buzzes with ideas, which are deeply embedded in the workflow, or completely focused on having fun.

As many of the staff are in and out of the office on a regular basis, or work remotely, a member of staff instigated a lunchtime show and tell session to keep everyone in touch with everything that was going on. The aim is to create a vibrant community with a degree of openness and understanding about what the priorities are and what is currently being worked on. And everyone can participate, regardless of where they happen to be based.

Ben Betts prefers to describe the culture that he has built in the company as problem-solving rather than learning, although learning is a critical element of it. It is fuelled by a commitment to openness. There are no walls, no offices or private spaces. Communications are easy and promote a sense of inclusiveness at all times. Even their financial statements are written up on a whiteboard showing current profit, performance and cash in hand.

There is also a core belief that it is important to speak regularly to those who work remotely. The company does not exclusively rely on email or Slack. Staff outside Oxford, including those in Boston, are spoken to every single day. That is where nuances are picked up, which may be invisible in written communications, and where real insights occur, and any problems are snuffed out quickly. It also indicates to those staff that are not based with the majority that they have not been forgotten by the core team in Oxford. No decisions are made, or strategies agreed, without broad discussion with everyone. There is no such thing as feeling remote or disconnected from the main flows of ideas or debates.

Alan and Ben spend over an hour a day on the phone or using Skype to talk to remote staff. They also stay in touch with each other. Every day, when possible, they organize a 45-minute walk/talk to catch up, and share challenges and insights. Indeed, reflection and walking are core elements of the culture. The company offices are located outside Oxford, in the countryside, so it is a pleasant environment in which to walk, reflect and think.

The company expects staff to define their own learning needs, and requests to enrol on a course or go to a conference are rarely turned down if those requests are reasonable and a good case can be made. The company believes that productivity and learning are directly related. This is reflected in Ben Betts' own experience. In his daily commute, he listens to podcasts and audiobooks. His tastes are broad and he makes a point of diving into industries a long way from his own, in order to track what is happening in business as a whole and not just the tech sector. He brings this broad perspective back into HT2.

The company culture emerged over time, and as that culture took root, Ben and Alan nurtured it carefully. Now there is a sense that it is firmly established, and it can more or less look after itself. This has enabled the bedrock that defines the company to be expressed by the company values, rather than in the personalities of key staff members. For example, not all the elements that are now considered central to the company necessarily came from Ben and Alan. Standing desks, for example, were a staff member's idea. The concept and the practice has now become embedded in the company and helps define the look and feel of the office.

HT2 has four core values. The first is 'customer success fanatics'. They care about their customers and want the projects that involve their software to be successful. The second is that the company is data and experience led. Decisions are data and experience driven and focused on maximum impact. The third is a bias towards action and results, rather than process. Finally, the company wants to be 'inspirational and fun to work with'. All four of the values are outward facing and clearly define the parameters of the customer experience.

HT2 has learning at its heart. It tries to be in tune with the latest ideas and not afraid to change if it needs to. In the same way that Happy Ltd pivots when the outside environment changes, HT2 would describe itself as having its ear to the ground in order that it can pick up distant rumbles and react fast.

A conversation with Emma Sephton, product manager at HT2

Emma has worked for HT2 for 16 months. In that time, she has moved from a project manager role (her background) in the company to product manager in charge of HT2's latest product: Red Panda. She has a Higher Education background. Having spent four years at the University of Warwick she was ready to move into a different work environment. What she likes about the company is the fact that it is open and focuses on learning and development. No one is bracketed or pigeonholed, and she loves the vision and passion demonstrated by her colleagues. There is a sense that there are no barriers. You are allowed to do your job and have your eye on other jobs you might want to move in to. She feels that she has a voice and her views are respected, and the company is supportive and helpful. She finds this stimulating and motivating. She has no regrets about the move from a large, stable and secure institution to a small, higher-risk company.

Her preparation for the transition to product manager was managed by the Slack community. She started as a lurker in the external 'mind the product' community, and then began to participate, by asking relevant questions. Finally, she attended a workshop for new product managers. It meant that she was eased into the new role gently, and still has a sense of excitement about guiding a brand-new product into the market and helping make it a success. She feels the benefits of the high-trust culture where she has been supported, but she is driving forward under her own steam.

Her initial sense of excitement when she joined the company has never gone away. The openness and commitment of all those around her means that her role is never monotonous and she continues to learn at pace. The research side of the company was very familiar to her, but the software dimension was an entirely new area that she had to learn.

If she had to make one distinction between her previous employer (the University) and HT2, it would be that, previously, not knowing was frowned upon. Not knowing made you feel incompetent and was consequently best concealed. In this company, she felt that she did not have to prove herself, and admitting what she did not know was welcomed, because it gave people the opportunity to share, support and help her get better.

The atmosphere is very informal and that deep integration of work and of learning is hugely valued by Emma. For her, learning is work, and work is learning. There are formal opportunities to learn and gain qualifications but most of what goes on is informal learning. This is everywhere all the time. She finds this aspect of the culture extremely energizing and motivating.

She rates herself, now, as a more effective learner than when she joined the company in spite of having worked in a University. She is naturally resourceful and has exploited her ability to be curious and ask good questions. She has discovered a very simple truth, which is that everyone *actually* likes the chance to help if they are given the opportunity to do so.

She believes that HT2 demonstrates a learning culture in action. There is a symbiotic relationship between the staff, linked by learning, and lubricated by the constant interactions on Slack. She works in an organization she hugely respects, with people she admires. She feels strongly motivated inside the company and is convinced that what drives that is the constant opportunity to learn, coupled with never being stifled or ignored. She is aware that she is growing intellectually and taking on challenges she never thought that she would have had the opportunity to tackle. Ironically, in HT2, being able to say 'I don't know' is the biggest source of discussion, challenge and energy.

Conclusions

The WD-40 Company has much in common with these two younger organizations. All three focus on a culture of coaching and development rather than management and control. One of the core precepts of them all is: 'do not tell when you can ask.' And curiosity and exploration are encouraged, or even demanded.

Happy Ltd and HT2 are also committed to building a good work/life balance. Both try to match how everyone does their job with how they run their life, and no one is expected to sacrifice the latter for the former. What staff learn is not narrowly focused on the business, it can span virtually any area of interest. The emphasis is on developing the individual in order to bring expertise and enthusiasm into the organization. And both organizations deliberately make space to allow this to happen. Thinking is actively encouraged.

In a recent *Harvard Business Review* article (2017), the marketing expert Denise Lee Yohn made a startlingly obvious point about organizational culture and its relationship to the organization brand, which others had missed. Her research concluded that:

It's having a distinct corporate culture – not a copycat of another firm's culture – that allows these great organizations to produce phenomenal results. Each of these companies has aligned and integrated its culture and brand to create a powerful engine of competitive advantage and growth. Their leaders understand that a strong, differentiated company culture contributes to a strong, differentiated brand – and that an extraordinary brand can support and advance an extraordinary culture.

The companies that she is referring to are Amazon and GE. The Happy Company and HT2 may not operate on the same global scale, but they do illustrate the powerful synergy of brand aligned to company culture. This alignment makes them stand out against their competitors and gives them a reputation and a status beyond their size. They are both more widely known and talked about than many companies much larger than they are. They both have a reputation for delivering, and for fair dealing and high ethical standards as well as for excellent staff whom you can trust.

Does being happy at work align to a learning culture?

The Happy Manifesto by Henry Stewart defines the 10 core behaviours that Happy Ltd lives by and which Stewart claims made the difference that separates Happy from a thousand other organizations. It forms the core of the work that the company does, which is to help other organizations build better workplaces. The manifesto is the source code for developing more engaged and less toxic workplaces.

The 10 elements of the manifesto can be referenced back to the core elements of the cultures of Happy Ltd and HT2. The first is probably the most important of the 10. It is 'enable people to work at their best.' This is a driving part of the ethos of both companies and is in stark contrast to many organizations, where that concept is very far down the list of priorities: nice to have but set aside by other priorities, and therefore almost completely invisible. If people work at their best, organizations can achieve more and be more effective. The opposite is also true: disengaged staff working sub-optimally achieve less, make more mistakes and care less about what they deliver.

The second element relates to the first and is to 'enable your people to feel good'. In Stewart's eyes, the key focus for any manager is to help his or her people feel good about themselves, and to create an environment that encourages that. It also means giving staff the benefit of the doubt, taking time to understand what drives them and what difficulties and challenges they face, as well as creating a work environment that is open, flexible and fun. That does not imply undemanding. Both companies stretch and challenge their staff but in an environment that offers support.

This logic leads to the third element: 'creating a great workplace means good business sense.' The idea that empowered staff are more productive is true. There is clear evidence to show that organizations that bother to invest in their staff perform better over time than organizations that do not. Alex Edman's paper (2011) that was published while he was an academic at the Wharton School in University of Pennsylvania still stands as a seminal piece of research. It gathers rigorous evidence to prove that companies that invest in their staff outperform the stock market within their particular sector. This is data gleaned from tracking companies over 25 years. If anyone has any doubts about the financial upside of looking after people and building engagement, Edman's paper is essential reading.

The fourth element is 'freedom within clear guidelines'. Stewart's own research firmly convinced him that this is what the vast major-ity of staff want from work (Stewart, 2012). Stewart believes that staff should be given responsibility to complete their targets in ways that suit them, providing what is being demanded is reasonable. Micromanagement destroys good people and develops dysfunc-tional workplaces.

The drive for transparency extends into the next element, which is 'be open and transparent'. Without information, no one can take responsibility or make decisions. In Happy, all financial information is openly discussed at staff meetings. In HT2 the financial position of the company is written on a whiteboard in their main office. People take decisions in context. The result is they take better decisions that they own. It is easy to share the good news when things are going well but, as Stewart points out, it is more important to share financial information when things are going badly. If staff are aware of an issue, everyone can contribute to solving the problem. Openness also quashes the rumour mill and undermines negativity.

The sixth element is 'recruit for attitude, train for skill'. When I arrived at the BBC, I was shocked to discover that the company operated what they called a 'fair selection' policy. This meant that, when interviewing staff, the same questions were asked of each candidate, and they were scored on their responses, together with the skills and competences they had related to the job description. At the end of the process the candidate who received the highest score had to be offered the job, regardless of how well they might fit into the organization. Many disastrous appointments were made as a result! The organization shifted to a recruit for attitude, train for skill policy. This not only impacted the culture of the organization and was almost immediately visible. And all the time this policy was implemented, there were never skill deficits. Enthusiastic new recruits were quickly able to learn on the job and build their skills through coaching.

The seventh element is 'celebrate mistakes'. It is much more useful to own up to mistakes, and take responsibility for fixing them next time, than it is to create a culture of blame and buck passing. Both Happy and HT2 talk about mistakes as premium learning experiences not as firing offences.

The eighth element is 'community: create mutual benefit'. Both Happy and HT2 have to remain profitable to survive, but that is not the only reason for being in business. The bigger aspiration is to make a difference and a contribution to the greater good. Happy has sponsored some of its staff to visit developing countries in order to train trainers and leave behind a legacy of skills. HT2 has given away its resources to organizations or communities that cannot afford to buy them. Both companies encourage staff to volunteer in their communities, and time is allocated for it.

The ninth element is about work/life balance. Staff are encouraged to 'love their work, but also get a life!' Stewart (2012) argues that 'many businesses regard working late as a sign of commitment. It is just as likely to be a sign of poor organization, of too many meetings, and unnecessary activities during the day.'

This attitude towards work/life balance has parallels in HT2. Both organizations want their people to work smarter not harder. Both organizations start from the assumption that there is a normal working day, and a life beyond work. They then structure the work to fit rather than take over. Being too tired or too exhausted to do any more than fall into bed after a day's work is not just unacceptable but leads to attrition and a lack of commitment. Both CEOs sign up to minimizing that occurrence and encouraging people to go home!

The last piece of the Happy Manifesto jigsaw is to 'select managers who are good at managing.' What that means is that moving up through an organization does not necessarily have to mean becoming a manager. All of Happy's coordinators choose that route. Many of their most skilled staff, who are paid no less, have decided not to take on leadership roles. It is also true in HT2. Both organizations have flat team-based structures and the team coordinators emerge from the organization because they are good at that role, not because they have reached a specific level of seniority. It is not about promotion or pay level. Both organizations believe that a poor manager, or a reluctant manager, can do much more damage than good. The great managers clear the way, enable staff to perform at their best, and take great pride in developing the people they work with. A willingness to do that is the key criterion for selection.

A learning culture is a by-product and a contributor to a healthy workplace culture, and also a way of holding that workplace culture to account. This logic links the Henry Stewart book to a recent *Harvard Business Review* press publication called 'How to be Happy at Work' by the University of Pennsylvania academic, Dr Annie McKee. Like Stewart, McKee believes that being happy at work is attainable for everybody and is not an impossible illusion: 'Cultivating happiness at work is a deliberate, conscious act. You know what it takes: finding and living your purpose, focusing patiently on your future, building meaningful friendships' (McKee, 2017: 187).

But to move from the individual to the collective requires a strong, resonant organizational culture. It is about building a sense of purpose and a vision for the future, but it is equally about making each job meaningful and making each member of staff feel valued and respected. Virtually all the elements that McKee lists as part of a resonant culture have strong learning at their heart.

In exactly the same way, most of the elements of a toxic culture at some point discourage learning, remove motivation and deny insight. At the heart of the resonant culture, McKee claims is 'respect for the individual's right to grow and develop' (McKee, 2017: 190). At the heart of a toxic culture is inequity, disrespect and a clear sense of injustice. You need to choose where you would rather work.

What are the key lessons that you can take away?

1 Culture is driven from the top, but it has to be lived right through the organization without exception for a learning culture to flourish.

2 Learning emerges best from an overall culture of mutual interdependence, helpful enquiry and constant debate.

3 Motivated and engaged staff are loyal staff, and care about the company, their customers and their colleagues.

4 Work/life balance is a key element for maintaining freshness and energy in the organization. Nothing much gets done well when everyone is worn out. Curiosity and problem solving require fresh minds to operate successfully.

5 Teams and individuals are coached rather than managed. This allows self-management to emerge as a powerful organizational principle. Both organizations stress the need to help their teams become as autonomous as possible.

6 A key element of a vibrant learning culture is the confidence and willingness of staff to share work in progress. In other words, to 'work out loud'. Both sets of staff share what they are doing, share their challenges, and ask for help when they need to.

7 Constant and honest communication across the organization is very important. Everyone has a voice and is treated with respect.

8 Both organizations have a no blame culture, and no one is punished for making mistakes.

9 Attention is paid to the physical layout and the look and feel of their offices. Both companies are open plan, and the layout encourages people to talk to each other, rather than email across the room.

10 Everyone has a voice, and everyone feels that they are listened to. The collective is important, but individuals matter too.

11 Innovation bubbles up from all around both organizations. There is no monopoly on great ideas, and leaders listen and learn as a result.

References

Covey, S M R (2006) *The Speed of Trust: The one thing that changes everything*, Free Press, pp 287–296

Edmans, A (2011) Does the stock market fully value intangibles? Employee satisfaction and equity prices, *Journal of Financial Economics*, **101** (3), pp 621–640

Guardian (2016) Newspaper co-founder: 'We raised £6.5m... and lost it all in six weeks', *Guardian*, 19 September 2016

Lee Yohn, D (2017) Why your company culture should match your brand, *Harvard Business Review*, 26 June 2017

McKee, A (2017) *How to be Happy at Work*, Harvard Business Review Press, Harvard

Stewart, H (2012) *The Happy Manifesto: Make your organisation a great place to work – now!* Happy/Kogan Page, London

PART THREE
Building a learning culture: a gyroscope for organizational effectiveness

Work and learning

07

Lynda Gratton, the London Business School academic and co-author of the best-selling book *The 100-Year Life* (Gratton and Scott, 2016), published an article in the *MIT Sloan Management Review* in March 2018 (Gratton, 2018) that focuses on why business leaders should prepare their staff for rapid and significant changes in the nature of work. She claims that employees are anxious and ill-prepared for the technological and social changes that will revolutionize work and impact virtually all their roles over the next 5 to 10 years. Extending learning is a critical part of the armour to protect people from future obsolescence. She claims:

> One of the fundamental outcomes of the intersection of technological innovations and increasing longevity is that one-off early education will not be sufficiently strong enough to propel people through their whole working lives. People will need to engage in work that has development opportunities built into it, be prepared to spend some of their leisure time upskilling, and probably take significant chunks of time out of work to learn a new skill. (Gratton, 2018)

The book that she wrote with fellow London Business School academic Andrew Scott makes much the same point about the primacy of learning:

> Across a long productive life there will be an increasing focus on general portable skills and capabilities such as *mental flexibility and agility* [Gratton's emphasis]. This raises an interesting conflict between this need for general skills and the importance of valuable specialization. (Gratton and Scott, 2016: 74–75)

Those who have read this book up until now will welcome Gratton's words but recognize that a learning culture is far more than 'development opportunities' and skill acquisition, however important those concepts are.

In the face of new working conditions and new jobs, the learning described by Gratton is still focused on conventional models. The revolution in work needs to be paralleled by a revolution in learning. The operation of learning culture, as part of the day-to-day working processes, brings work and learning closer and closer together, to the point where they are indistinguishable.

The focus I have described, for example in the WD-40 Company of having constant sharing of insight, and an analysis of what works and what does not, begins to close the gap between what is a specific and identifiable work skill, and what is mental flexibility and agility. Indeed, Gillian Pillans told us in Chapter 3 that operational learning (day-to-day skill development) has to be complemented by generative learning, which is about specific processes that help build thinking and process skills and develop agility and flexibility. They do not contradict one another in the learning organization because they both emerge from the workflow and happen informally as well as formally.

In order to really be prepared to face the future of work, learning has to become almost instinctive and inclusive. There should be much less time for learning separated from work, but much more time for learning as part of work. The focus ought to be on work, and how to make work more effective. That is less about individual roles and more on work as a whole. In other words, concentrating on the organization and what needs to be done for it to thrive.

A model for the development of a learning organization

The Harvard academics David Garvin and Amy C Edmondson wrote a *Harvard Business Review* article in March 2008 asking the simple question: is yours a learning organization?

David Garvin is discussed earlier in this book as the author of a sceptical article on Senge's promise to deliver learning organizations. He was concerned about the complexity of the Senge model. Twenty years later the business environment is much more complex and the need to move forward is acute. Garvin has answered his earlier questions and produced a framework that is designed to help readers answer the question that frames the article: is yours a learning organization?

The authors observe that the pressure on organizations increases, but the clarity about what to do to create a learning organization is still hard to find. They fill the gap by arguing:

> Organizations need to learn more than ever as they confront these mounting forces. Each company must become a learning organization. The concept is not a new one. It flourished in the 1990s, stimulated by Peter M. Senge's The Fifth Discipline and countless other publications, workshops and websites. The result was a compelling vision of an organization made up of employees skilled at creating, acquiring, and transferring knowledge. These people could help their firms cultivate tolerance, foster open discussion, think holistically and systematically.
> (Garvin, Edmondson and Gino, 2008: 1)

The article argues that the great idea from the 1990s is still waiting for its time to come. The original prescriptions were too vague to be implemented successfully, the authors argue, so they have proposed their own model with three key building blocks. The first of these was 'a supportive learning environment'. This has four features that define what this means in practice. These are all cultural aspects: the first two are psychological safety, coupled with an appreciation for and a tolerance of differences, and then an openness to new ideas, and finally allowing time for reflection.

The second building block is 'concrete learning processes and practices'. They argue that 'knowledge must be shared in systematic and clearly defined ways'.

Finally, the last building block is 'leadership that reinforces learning'.

These are their conditions for a learning organization and they have devised a number of instruments that organizations can use to test out their readiness and work out how far they still need to go to become learning organizations. This list is close to the four conditions listed in this book and the article offers no contradictory conclusions to mine or takes the reader in a different direction. The point they make is the point this book makes: we need practical agendas that are neither too complex, nor too one dimensional to work, and that a learning organization emerges when more than one condition is met. Their three building blocks are not optional; each is important: the creation of a supportive learning environment allows concrete learning processes and practices to be established but this will not happen without leadership that reinforces learning.

It is clear that there is a need to work on the organization to build these conditions, as well as a need to work on learning to make it more effective. Is that enough though?

A model devised by Peppe Auricchio from IESE Business School builds a picture of how a learning organization might operate, using a simple graphic which helps explain the overall environment that creates the conditions for learning. His conclusions emerge from a series of debates and discussion about the nature of innovation in organizations, and specifically the nature of innovation in learning, which he had organized within the Business School, IESE. The model is still in development, and I am grateful to Dr Auricchio, who is charged with building innovation in IESE, for permission to use this nascent model (see Figure 7.1).

The model comprises two interlocking circles. The inner circle is essentially the engine that drives the outer circle. The inner circle establishes the big organizational drivers that are fundamental building blocks for any kind of learning organization. This inner circle defines the vision for learning, the attitudes that are required by the staff that are recruited, and finally the behaviours expected of everyone in order to create the right climate for shared learning to flourish. These are the basic prerequisites of a learning organization.

The outer circle defines the nature of the learning that emerges as a product of the conditions elaborated in the inner circle. The outer circle argues for a kind of learning that is continuous and integrated into the day-to-day processes and practices of work. It should also be learner led; in other words, something that everybody is responsible for, not something done to the majority by a small minority. Learning has to be owned, embedded in the workflow and continuous.

The third element is the contextual one. It is exemplified in the regular question used by employees of the WD-40 Company when they meet: 'what did you learn today?' (see Chapter 5). The organization, as a whole, seeks out learning moments and ensures that the insights are shared, rather than hoarded or siloed. This implies a different attitude towards dealing with issues and challenges.

The idea is that failure is seen as a learning moment rather than an excuse to blame, and requires a different kind of conversation and a different approach. Conversations cease to be limited exclusively to the success of an individual project, but an exploration of the learning that emerged. The organization has to ensure that it has both a culture that encourages openness together with the right processes in place to both store the learning and distribute it widely around the organization so it can be used as a reference point to help define future action.

The final element is that learning should be data-driven. This means that, like virtually every element in modern-day business, learning is enriched by a torrent of data that defines what, how and when learning has taken place, and how to optimize the learning experience for each individual, as well as providing a dashboard to illustrate what is happening across the whole organization. Rich learning data can offer holistic snapshots of what is being learned and shared across the whole organization at any moment, as well as supporting individual learning by suggesting learning pathways and encouraging engagement and sharing.

Data can be used to help individuals determine what they need and, rather like Netflix, suggest what should be or could be the next stage in the learning journey. This process allows deep personalization so that each individual is offered a unique pathway. That individualized data can be collated to give the organization a snapshot of what is going on in teams, groups or across the whole company. This means that the learning organization has a clear view of what is going on that can reveal where learning gaps or performance pain points exist. It also reveals any misalignment between skills and tasks. Seamless evolution of workflow is therefore possible.

This model is dynamic. For example, the behaviours and attitudes of staff will change in the light of the learning in which they are engaged. Action can be coordinated when the data determines that there are skills gaps, or poor performance is revealed. In addition, this is learning in context. The focus of attention is the workflow, the business environment or changing markets and emerging needs.

Figure 7.1   An organization that learns: Framework for discussion

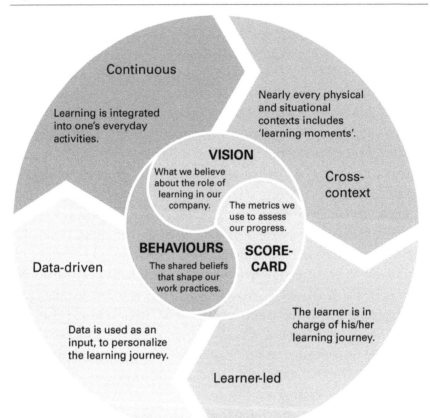

Reproduced with permission

To counter technological disruption, for example, an organization requires a fast, collective response, and agreement about what has to happen in order to survive. It is easier to marshal resources to work on problems, and easier to action any resulting conclusions. You can almost picture this model as the wheel of my organizational gyroscope (see Chapter 1). And like a gyroscope, the stability and accuracy only occurs when the wheel has velocity. The continuous action of the wheel generates energy and allows a constant view of the business horizon. Auricchio's model, as a consequence, is not static, but dynamic. The two wheels work together and generate insights on a continuous basis.

How do we understand a learning culture?

We need to understand the concept of a learning culture in a different way to a learning organization. I have suggested a new model to illuminate that process. A learning organization determines a strong learning culture. Building a learning culture allows a learning organization to emerge. The two are interlocked.

The model is a combination of the forces that pressure an organization from outside, together with the conditions that are required inside the organization to neutralize those forces, and maintain equilibrium. The external environment is increasingly volatile and uncertain. Those two factors provide the opportunity for challenging what currently exists and disrupting what appear to be secure incumbents in a market place. In the face of that pressure, organizations have to react intelligently. It is hard to be on top of that constant change, and impossible for a small leadership cohort to have all the answers.

It is the power of the whole organization that provides the solutions, and the ability to react fast to changing circumstances ensures survival. This volatility, uncertainty, disruption and challenge impact different organizations in different ways, but essentially the response has to involve some kind of reframing of the problem, which allows a repositioning of the organization. This can be a series of minor checks and changes, or a transformation of the entire organization.

In the light of the massive digital disruption occurring in manufacturing, for example, an organization as huge as GE has repositioned itself as 'The Digital Industrial Company', which emphasizes that digital technologies can add significant value to the design, development and manufacture of engineering products such as locomotives, jet engines and power plants (www.GE.com).

To ensure that this was not just empty words, huge numbers of core staff had to engage around what a digital industrial company did differently. It also involved a new generation of software engineers getting to know their more traditional engineering counterparts, and learning to work together productively. Those issues, challenges and potential disruptions have to be recognized but brought inside the organization, in order to work out what to do. This requires collaboration, diversity of approach and enormous respect as well as trust for those trying to work out what to do next.

Explaining the model

The outer layer of the model indicates the nature of the external environment. The next layer shows the fundamental behaviours that can manage the external environment and build the conditions for the learning to take place. The third layer describes the culture of learning that is at the heart of the model.

The underpinning value is trust, which emerges from a leadership process that is designed to enhance team performance and build engagement and commitment. This impacts staff at all levels of the organization. The outcome of that leadership process is an empowered and engaged workforce. Only when this exists can the core behaviours that drive a learning culture – sharing, collaborating with appropriate autonomy and clear purpose – emerge.

These are core values and behaviours that determine how the organization reacts to that external layer of turbulence. This is the bedrock of a learning culture. It creates permeable layers in the organization. This permeability allows insight from outside to be analysed and processed in multiple locations inside, using the diverse skills and knowledge of the entire workforce.

Permeability across the organization allows the best people to collaborate regardless of where they work, and that common cause is the key to successful problem solving. Without this permeability, problems are not recognized until too late, and insight does not emerge fast enough or widely enough across the organization. It is, consequently, worth spending a significant amount of time developing the right empowering leadership, to build and sustain a high level of trust and an engaged and happy workforce.

It is possible to develop high levels of collaboration, widespread sharing of insight, and an urgent sense of purpose that is widely shared inside an organization. But this requires a high level of trust and autonomy, as well a culture where asking for help and admitting what you do not know is normative.

Figure 7.2 How an organization reacts to turbulence

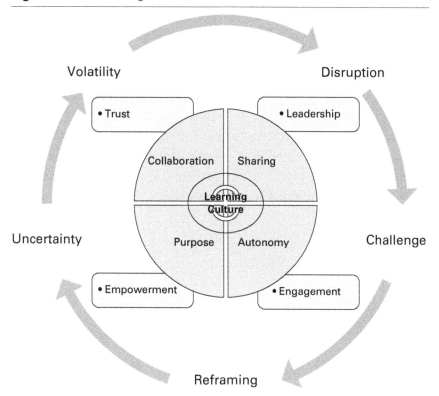

Autonomy needs boundaries and clarity about what can be decided upon at what level. Henry Stewart in his Happy Manifesto describes this attribute as: 'freedom within clear guidelines' (Stewart, 2012: 54–57). It is complex and always easier to just say no, but as a process where people move forward piece by piece, taking more responsibility as their experience grows, it is second to none at building motivation and engagement. It can only work, however, if empowerment is coupled with significant support and smart trust. This builds a model of continuing growth and development for individuals and an overall increase in competency and authority for the organization. It is action through enquiry and experimentation. Learning is always the product of this process.

Given trust, empowering leadership, autonomy and engaged staff who are encouraged to share and collaborate on a profound level, the culture that emerges is strongly allied to learning and improving.

Therefore, each one of the elements listed in the model is extremely important. Together they form a fragile ecosystem, and it requires care and nurture to sustain it. Again, the metaphor of the organizational gyroscope is pertinent. The energy generated by those processes, and the energy generation by driving forward with a clear purpose and direction, helps maintain a clear sight of the horizon, regardless of the volatility and lack of clarity in the external environment.

These processes represent large commitments for anyone taking the ideas in this book into their organizations. Therefore, in the final chapter, those large blocks of activity are broken down into smaller steps that can be more easily implemented.

References

Garvin, D A, Edmondson, A C and Gino, F (2008) Is yours a learning organization? *Harvard Business Review*, March 2008

Gratton, L (2018) How leaders face the future of work, *MIT Sloan Management Review*, 19 March 2018: https://sloanreview.mit.edu/article/how-leaders-face-the-future-of-work/

Gratton, L and Scott, A (2016) *The 100-Year Life: Living and working in an age of longevity*, Bloomsbury, London

Stewart, H (2012) *The Happy Manifesto*, Happy Publishing

Why technology 08 is an essential component of a learning culture

Any sufficiently advanced technology is indistinguishable from magic. (Rodney Brooks)

Setting the scene

In 2016 the *Washington Post* published an e-book called *Generation Z: What it's like to grow up in the age of likes, LOLs, and longing* (Contrera and Gibson, 2016). It is one of a series of essays by *Washington Post* journalists, giving staff the time and space to do some detailed research and record it in long-form publications. It was also an additional nugget of content designed to lure new readers to subscribe to the electronic version of the newspaper. There is now a collection of 15 or more of the *Post*'s e-books, covering contentious issues that could benefit from long-form exposition. This book has a very simple and clear focus: to understand better those born around the year 2000, in particular their tech habits.

The main conclusion from this brief essay is that: 'Researchers have found that the shift experienced by today's teens is unprecedented. Every facet of their lives – education, friendship, romance, careers – will be shaped by the technology in their hands. We wanted to understand exactly what it means to grow up in this new era – and wanted to understand it through their eyes' (Contrera and Gibson, 2016: 4).

The book shows that the technology is not just a significant part of these young people's social lives but much more. It is the means to access homework from school, post assignments and build reports, as well as access research and information. Their phone is both 'official', as the portal into their learning world, and 'social', the main way of keeping in touch with friends: 'Even when their phones aren't out, kids chat about what's going on online... and the kids without technology can't even engage in the conversation' (Contrera and Gibson, 2016: 57).

It is a private environment (limited to the group) that shuts out parents and other adults, and it can be cruel and hurtful but also exhilarating. It is a world entirely mediated by technology. It is, consequently, the way that this group works, the way the group learns as well as the way they socialize. And this generation are now moving out of the school system into universities or colleges. They will be entering the workforce in the next two to three years. They are not a weird aberration compared to the rest of humanity. They simply represent the next logical step towards dependence on and the embracing of technology. When you have the equivalent of a supercomputer in your pocket that is connected wirelessly to everyone else's, and allows almost frictionless activity, it makes sense to use it extensively. This is the first 100 per cent connected generation and they are pointing the way to the future. If we ignore this simple truth, we are ignoring strong and helpful signals.

The advent of ubiquitous pocket- or purse-based technology will inevitably shape not just leisure and social interaction but work itself. The workplace cannot remain an oasis of technological incompetence and complexity. It will catch up to the expectations that are established in the rest of people's lives. We are still at an early stage of that technology transformation. It will be both disruptive and significant. It is impossible to engage, realistically, in any discussion about the use of technology, and the impact of technology on the development of a learning culture, without a clear understanding of the extent and nature of that transformation.

There is a story told by Jonny Ive at Steve Jobs' memorial service. It recounts a morning when Jobs burst into Ive's design lab asking about the efficiency of various animals in locomotion. This was information that Jobs had gleaned from the *Scientific American*. He went on:

I read a study that measured the efficiency of locomotion for various species on the planet. The condor used the least energy to move a kilometre. And humans came in with a rather unimpressive showing, about a third of the way down the list. It was not too proud a showing for the crown of creation. So, that didn't look so good. But then somebody at *Scientific American* had the insight to test the efficiency of locomotion for a man on a bicycle. And a man on a bicycle, a human on a bicycle, blew the condor away, completely off the top of the charts. And that's what a computer is to me. What a computer is to me is the most remarkable tool that we've ever come up with, and it's the equivalent of a bicycle for our minds. (www.bikeboom.info/efficiency)

In many ways Jobs' insight is brilliant; the advent of the personal computer in the work sphere has yielded a dramatic increase in productivity for all those who use it. It is now an integral part of all knowledge work, with only a few people able to function at work without access to information technology. Now, however, what works on a large, often clunky laptop or desktop computer will run equally smoothly on the device in your pocket. This shift to smartphone and tablet capability is as big an advance as the advent of the personal computer.

This is partly due to the increased flexibility and portability offered by the new device but more specifically it is due to its ubiquity. Most people come to work with a smartphone in their pocket or purse (an article in *The Economist* in 2015 claimed that 'the supercomputer in your pocket' will be owned by 80 per cent of the world's population by 2020). No one was taught to use it, and yet it is a completely integral part of most people's lives, and is the unifying factor between work and leisure, often used equally for both. I remember being staggered 10 years ago when I opened the box and took out my first iPhone to discover that the instruction manual was a single, small phone-size sheet of paper. It said, simply, 'connect your phone to your laptop and open iTunes'. That compared to the horrific 200-page plus nightmare of a manual for my previous phone, where every apparently simple action has endless steps and involved navigating through hundreds of menu items.

Those organizations that see the potential offer their staff the opportunity to use and be paid to use their own device rather than one (often less functional) supplied by the company. There are huge cost savings and efficiencies to be gained by integrating and exploiting the familiarity and comfort people feel using their personal technology for their work.

We are only dimly glimpsing the extraordinary impact this will have on what we do, and how we do it. We could be on the cusp of a startling shift that if managed well will make our lives easier, and make work more efficient, familiar and enjoyable. If we do it badly, there will be a clear and ongoing tension with our increasingly sophisticated and connected leisure time, which will contrast badly with the clumsy, clunky, inefficient and inconvenient technologies that we will be forced to continue to use at work.

If we are going to discuss learning culture, technology and digital disruption have to be somewhere at the heart of this discussion. This aspect is the major differentiator between the debates about the role of workplace learning in the 1980s and the way we discuss it now. Any attempt to move forward without fully embracing the learning potential of technology, and acknowledging the massive leaps forward that artificial intelligence will make to the process of personalizing and supporting the learning needs of all employees in the workplace, would be to do this topic a grave disservice.

In many ways the states of technology development and organization development are moving at a similar place. Our potential in these areas, the opportunity of exploit exciting new technologies and organizational structures, lags behind our skills and the capacity of our organizations to change. This idea is encapsulated in the 2014 book by Erik Brynjolfsson and Andrew McAfee, *The Second Machine Age*.

The inflection point has been reached

The venture capitalist Jason Palmer (ex Kaplan University, Ex Bill and Melinda Gates Foundation) described the evolution of technology for learning in a blog post published in May 2017. The focus is mainly schools, but the logic is more broadly applicable. He divides up the evolution of what he calls 'educational technology' into a number of key stages. Stage one lasted from 1993 to 2004. Palmer calls it the 'infrastructure era' when everyone built out internet access, and Learning Management systems were created to manage the distribution of online programmes and collect rudimentary data on their performance. Stage two he dated from 2004 to 2011 and tracks the growth of online learning and the beginnings of data gathering and data analytics. The third stage he calls 'From Early Adopters to Mainstream Adoption' and will run from 2011–2020. We are approaching the end of that stage now. Learning technologies are in the mainstream, and the growth of online learning has bifurcated into many different streams of synchronous and asynchronous engagement, using a bewildering variety of new technologies.

This inflection moment that has triggered the new stage (Palmer's fifth stage), is due to a number of integrated factors: organizations have sufficient infrastructure to carry high-resolution information seamlessly across the whole organization; and both organizations and individuals have appropriate devices that are so freely available as to be ubiquitous, such as laptops, tablets and smartphones. The next chapter, which begins imminently, will have the luxury of all that hardware resource, together with new kinds of software and new ideas to draw upon. The technology environment and its immediacy and significance will be dramatically enhanced.

Palmer concludes by saying that he is 'optimistic about the next decade of educational technology and innovation.' He implies that the hard work has been done, and now is the time to reap the rewards of perseverance. There is much evidence to support Palmer's assertion. This is provided by analysts such as Bersin (www.bersin.com) and Gartner (https://www.gartner.com/technology/topics/trends.jsp) in the United States, and Fosway (www.fosway.com) and Towards Maturity (https://towardsmaturity.org) in the United Kingdom, who support the idea that a great leap forward is not just possible but inevitable. The nature of that shift is caused by the conjunction of sophisticated software algorithms, unlimited storage provided by the Cloud, and enormous processing power that resides in both hand-held devices as well as powerful computers. This next stage in learning technology will cause huge disruption and challenge our assumptions about what, when and how learning will take place, and this mirrors the digital disruption occurring in many industries and almost every workplace.

There is a range of dominant features for this next stage, but a crucial underpinning of much of these developments is provided by machine intelligence, the internet of things, and the disruption caused by new powerful apps that act as platforms that will redefine the user experience. Think Airbnb, which has disrupted the hotel market without owning a single room, and Uber that has transformed the taxi industry without owning a single car or employing a single driver. These are only possible because cheap ubiquitous applications allow, not an improvement of what exists, but a complete rethink of what infrastructure is necessary and how you can manage services on a global scale. The learning industry is huge and as susceptible to technological disruption as any other.

Machine intelligence: algorithms and personalization

In a recent edition of *The Economist* (2017) it is claimed that Artificial Intelligence (AI) was the new attractive investment target:

> Two letters can add up to a lot of money. No area of technology is hotter than AI. Venture-capital investment in AI in the first nine months of 2017 totalled $7.6 bn, according to Pitchbook, a data provider; that compares with full-year figures of $5.4 bn in 2016. In the year to date, there have been $21.3 bn in AI related M&A deals, around 26 times more than in 2015.

AI is transforming businesses as software helps machines learn from their experience of the world and work out, independently of human intervention, what actions to take or draw conclusions about preferences or needs. Facebook and Google have immensely powerful algorithms that determine what you see (and what adverts are put in front of you). The more time you spend on Google or Facebook, the better they know you, the more accurate their suggestions of content. Netflix shows each subscriber only a fraction of the content that they have rights to, so you do not drown in empty suggestions of useless materials. The choices are based on what you have watched and what you have explored. It takes away the hassle of searching, or being offered thousands of irrelevant choices. The ethical issues around data mining and use of personal information are all around us. This is high on everyone's agenda due to the debate in 2018 about how Facebook uses and sells its customers' personal data or allows third-party companies to mine Facebook's personal data and sell it on to third parties as a marketing service. A huge amount has been written on this but see, as an example, *Fortune Magazine* (2018).

If Netflix operated like a conventional learning management system, it would present you with an undiscriminating list of films and TV shows with a poor interface, and would be no more helpful the thousandth time you used it, than it was the first time.

Yet the possibility of a Netflix for learning is abundantly practical, and a powerful step towards user control and user-initiated action, or at least a combination of informed, curated choices for the learner and personalized recommendations by the employer. It could seamlessly deliver a personalized set of learning opportunities that encourage participation and exploration, as well as stimulating agility and curiosity.

There is a lot of hysteria generated by a media industry anxious to have us believe that machine intelligence in general, and robots in particular, will take half our jobs in 10 to 20 years' time. The evidence of this has been brilliantly undermined by Rodney Brooks in an *MIT Technology Review* article of 2017 (Brooks, 2017: 62). His rational and data-based approach warns us to 'Watch out for argument about future technology that is magical. Such an argument can never be refuted. It is a faith-based argument, not a scientific argument.'

Although if we return to the original 2013 article published by Oxford University about job losses to automation, the evidence is harder to dismiss, although it is prediction not fact (Frey and Osborne, 2013). The model that is used to determine the potential job losses is highly complex and therefore hard to whole-heartedly endorse or refute. What Brooks does is treat more sceptically the Oxford data that others have picked up and circulated without questioning. Brooks looks for the evidence that AI and robots will destroy jobs and there is scant evidence of current disruption.

In the context described above, AI in learning, far from destroying jobs, will secure employment by helping individuals stay skilled and on top of evolving job roles, as well as preparing people for entirely new roles. What is the fundamental transformation of learning that parallels the disruption caused to taxi industry by Uber? The answer is personalization.

A key deliverable of machine intelligence in learning is the ability to personalize what is on offer. This is already evident to every subscriber of Facebook. The home page of each one of Facebook's 2.07 billion users is uniquely generated and based on user activity: one size fits one (www.statista.com/statistics/264810/number-of-monthly-active-facebook-users-worldwide).

Of the five AI trends that Ben Lorica, the Chief Data Scientist at O'Reilly Media, predicts in 2018, three of them involve more sophisticated and deeper learning emerging from both hardware and software improvements. His list is:

- substantial progress in machine learning methods, understanding, and pedagogy;
- new developments and lowered costs in hardware;
- developer tools for AI and deep learning will continue to evolve;
- many more use cases for automation; and
- concerns about privacy, ethics and responsible AI will continue to be addressed.

These will enable the fine-tuning and more accurate analysis of learning needs or gaps in competence and performance. The emerging ethical issues, Lorica believes, will be dealt with systematically. These are clearly higher on the list of priorities than the time that the post was written. The conclusion is that machine learning will permeate all aspects of life in an organization, including learning. This is difficult to dismiss.

Learning and media distribution models converge

The analyst Josh Bersin keeps a watchful eye on emerging technologies in both HR and corporate learning. In a March 2017 post in Forbes.Com (Bersin, 2017) he described the emergence of 'a new learning architecture' that represents a step change away from the use of Learning Management Systems (LMS) as the main way to distribute learning and gather data about its impact.

He notes that the technological disruption that has swept through a wide range of companies and processes has finally reached corporate learning. The dominant LMS, which stored, served and recorded learning for nearly 20 years, he predicts, will be replaced by a whole raft of new tools that will allow organizations to remake their digital learning infrastructure in a far more user-friendly and personalized way. I have tried to codify this massive shift in Table 8.1.

Table 8.1 Remaking digital learning infrastructure

Learning management system	New learning architecture
Monolithic and inflexible	Small scale and flexible
Exclusive and limited content	Inclusive and unlimited content
Poor user interface	User-friendly with defined and clear interface
List based on proprietary content	Selects and suggests individual pieces of learning
Content focus	Curation focus
Used mostly for compliance and formal courses	Open to incorporate all learning
Collects completion data on formal courses	Registers all learning including social learning and small chunks of learning from many sources
Ignores what exists 'out there'	Personalizes the learning experience
Unique and non-transferable file formats	Learns about the individual learner through use of systems
Media-unfriendly	Incorporates new learning environments and new media
Topic-driven	Encourages cooperation, debate and discussion
Aimed at mass learning for large groups who do similar work	Aimed to be a unique experience for each user
Data is provided for managers	Data is for individuals and amortized for the organization
Learning delivered at once	Spaced learning

In essence we are moving away from the massification of learning, which digital technologies allowed once we left a physical classroom setting and were able to digitize the learning experience, to a personalization of learning, using machine intelligence to curate and select what is appropriate for each individual at a specific point in time. The best analogy for this shift is to point to another industry that has already been through a similar disruption and therefore indicates the way forward for corporate learning. That is the media industry.

Previously, audiences searched through massive and clumsy electronic programming guides to work out what to view. Essentially the material was ordered by time of day and TV channel. If users had subscriptions for many channels, they had to scroll through hundreds of options to find out what they wanted to watch. And it was only possible to record programmes that were about to be transmitted rather than view anything that had already been transmitted.

This was a pretty awful, unfriendly experience and the interface was very hard to change. If you wanted to view only certain channels or certain channels at certain times, it was either impossible or very hard to work out how to do it. It did not matter if you never looked at a certain channel, or you looked at another one all the time, the software was completely unaware of this, and had no record of anything you did over time and therefore offered nothing back that reflected your experience and very limited customization. This got better over time, but the model was clunky and dominated by TV channels not programmes or preferences.

When Netflix came on the scene as a streamed service, the experience could not have been any more contrasting. No channels, low cost and an application that learns about you and what you watch, and suggests appropriate new content. The more you use the service, the better it gets at suggesting appropriate content. It also remembers where you got to in any single programme or any series and takes you back automatically to that point to continue your viewing. The interface is friendly and offers postage stamp images and brief synopses of what is available. And if more than one person accesses the same Netflix account, then it remembers each individual's preferences separately. So, for example, your children can access Netflix for Kids, which is an entirely separate suite of programmes and means that they cannot access inappropriate adult content. The software also learns their preferences, and suggests new programmes for them in exactly the way it does for their parents.

If all else fails, the user can search the massive database of content that is available. But this is a last resort. Nothing is scheduled. A whole series is often released at once, so that you can watch when you want, and how much you want, in any one session. The whole operation is centred around the user, and each Netflix account has a unique interface that registers the interests and viewing history of that user only. Apple TV has an app that amalgamates a number of your separate content subscriptions so that you can see your preferences and search across multiple providers in one operation. Compared to what went before, this is a breath of fresh air.

The BBC iPlayer has learned from this and offers a comprehensive viewing or listening experience through a single, friendly app. Live viewing (or listening) is possible across all BBC channels, but most programmes are also available to stream or download for up to a month after their initial transmission. However, it has limited intelligence and does not learn from previous activity, and what it suggests to the users is identical for everyone and, therefore, extremely hit or miss. The content can be presented as a huge list separated by theme and channel. But you can also order the content by type or by series. It represents a half-way house between an electronic programming guide and a Netflix-type experience. Now, many people no longer access the eight BBC TV channels terrestrially, but access live broadcast TV through the app. When you do this, it is possible to pause the live stream or go back to the start of a programme if you came in late. This must influence our consumption of learning.

The reality of our learning now is that when we want to learn something, we move from a YouTube video to a TED talk, to some structured more formal learning such as a MOOC (massive open online course). We may even pick up a book. We select according to the urgency and the topic. A MOOC is unlikely to help you fix your washing machine, and YouTube will not help you understand the traditions of modern architecture, for example, or complete a Master's course! But what we want, we want in a frame that looks tailored to our needs and is immediate.

Bersin identifies the various elements of the new learning architecture that he champions in the article mentioned above. On the one hand, he identifies software that is making a significant impact on organizations' ability to share, as it encourages employee networking, sharing of information and generally setting up conversations across geographies and across time. Examples include G suite, Microsoft teams, Slack and Workplace by Facebook. There is no clear winner – that is quite an important point. They appeal to different kinds of organizations, and there is a significant contrast between the way they operate and their scope.

Slack, for example, is designed to replace email communication between staff, and instead sets up threads of conversation within user-delineated and user-defined channels. This means that instead of an inbox crammed full of copies of emails where you respond to the sender, or to all of the recipients, Slack is visible to everyone given access to a channel. If you post a Slack message, all your fellow channel members have equal access. Slack is also completely agnostic in terms of what is posted. It handles video, audio messages, pictures, references as well as simple text. As a channel develops, it becomes a massive repository of shared learning. This software has been very popular in the technology community for example.

Facebook on the other hand has released an application that is designed to mimic its bigger brother. Workplace is simply a version of Facebook that is limited to a single workplace. It looks familiar, most people know how Facebook operates, and this means that they can use Workplace within seconds of being given access.

Facebook Workplace can replace or become the company intranet, while Slack reimagines email. There is no reason why they both cannot be used together, but Workplace tends to appeal to more traditional companies, as it offers a very fast way of building informal communities. Slack is designed to be more conversational and therefore more of an information and communication tool.

There are other programs that deliver learning in a different way. Companies such as Axonify and Practice help users develop their own skills. Axonify, for example, offers up small bites of learning on a regular basis to help the learner reinforce or develop new skills, whereas Practice allows the learner to rehearse his or her new knowledge or competency on video, and have that reviewed first by peers, and then, once revised, by experts. Neither would claim to offer a comprehensive learning service, but their role is to meet the important requirement to offer learning or information at the point of need and in small, targeted bite-size chunks.

More comprehensive software, such as Degreed, EdCast, PathGatherer (now merged with Degreed), and SAP Jam, curate and suggest learning for the individual based on job priorities or identified skills gaps. What they suggest can come from an almost infinite variety of sources. It does not matter whether it is internal or external content. It can be text, video, audio or even something highly structured such as a Massive Open Online Course, more commonly known as a MOOC. Those platforms keep a record of achievement, which can be focused on the individual, their cohort or team, or even the organization as a whole. And as the platforms are more extensively used, their algorithms work out what the individual needs and prefers, and they are able to suggest new, relevant resources for learning. The platform is a record store, a repository and an intelligent learning tutor, suggesting things you should learn, and encouraging you to move forward relentlessly in order to complete your learning tasks. This is why they are collectively referred to as learning experience platforms.

There are now applications that allow the corporate customer to develop formal learning programs using video or other resources and share those with staff. The software organizes the learning, keeps track of progress and encourages participation. Platforms include Intrepid, NovoEd, Curatr, EdX and Udemy. They help build a course not just resources; they all include space for discussion and query and, as digital learning environments, create engaging spaces to learn and they are accessible as asynchronous learning programmes or synchronous discussion and chat forums.

In the meantime, LinkedIn has acquired and integrated the learning platform Lynda, and rebranded it as LinkedIn Learning. Companies can buy in access to LinkedIn learning on behalf of their staff, and as it integrates into the LinkedIn profile, resources are targeted and relevant both to the individual and the employer.

All of this adds up to comprehensive and attractive offerings for staff that encourage curiosity, and help build the habit of constant learning, by suggesting relevant opportunities that focus both on job skills for today as well as future career skills for tomorrow. This is a long way removed from 'click through' compulsory e-learning that is designed to measure not much more than short-term memory, and has nothing to do with engagement or development.

The nature of the learning landscape

The learning landscape, in terms of technology, is becoming much more complex and fragmented. Just as everyone's smartphone is unique because the choice of apps is largely left to the individual, and therefore the permeations are almost infinite, the digital learning environment of a particular company can be a unique combination of applications that are configured in order to work for the organization and perhaps even given for the individual.

The purpose is to create something that is so engaging and relevant that it motivates learners to move forward at their own pace. It also sparks curiosity and allows individuals to explore and engage. Above all, it encourages conversations with peers in order to reinforce or extend the learning that is offered. We are such a long way from an individual sitting in front of the screen, bored by what they are forced to consume, that Bersin's claim that this is a revolution is not that far from the truth.

The critical point is that learning can be massively expanded by increasing its efficiency, rather than its volume, and that the conscious and articulated learning of the entire organization can be viewed and fine-tuned. We can begin to see how the idea of a learning culture is hugely enabled by an appropriate technology infrastructure to the point that now, it is impossible to separate a learning culture from the technologies that make it possible at scale.

What are the trends in technology?

In a recent webinar by Josh Bersin, he brought together his own data and that of Towards Maturity and their 2017 Bench Mark Study, together with Don Taylor's Learning Technology survey of 2017, and concluded that the top trending Technologies of 2017 were:

- user-generated content;

- experience and microlearning platforms such as Degreed, Fuel and Axonify;

- augmented reality – live situations overlaid with computer-generated content;

- virtual reality using headsets like Vive or Oculus Rift;

- artificial intelligence tools such as intelligent tutoring, virtual assistants like Alexa or Siri and chatbots.

These aspects of learning technology encourage and underpin a culture of learning and are encouraging the trend towards self-directed learning that is discussed above. Bersin claims that the use of self-directed learning has increased by 96 per cent, yet only 24 per cent of users considered their implementation had been successful. Taken together this marks a significant shift in the kind of technologies being used and the extent of their use, and recognizes that technology is at the heart of any kind of self-directed learning. It also foreshadows the increasing numbers of employees taking charge of their own development and careers and not waiting to be told what to do.

This is an area, as this book has shown, of experimentation and investment but still without clear direction or defined models emerging. But this will change rapidly as the external pressure to increase the amount of innovation and build business agility becomes unstoppable. This process involves all the people whom an organization employs in one way or another, not just full-time staff, but part-time staff, contractors, those in the gig economy, as well as suppliers and customers.

It is also clear that alumni are going to form an increasingly important group of potential reskilled and up-skilled returners to their former employers. Many organizations have set up alumni programmes to keep in touch with former employees that they value. It becomes increasingly likely that we will see a new kind of workforce emerging. This will comprise a workforce of people cycling through roles, sometimes as full-time staff, but also as contractors, short-time project workers, and even suppliers. No role will last for long as it will be project or activity focused, but the onus will increasingly be on the individual to stay relevant, and on the organization to stay in contact. Far from recruiting, essentially, strangers at great cost and risk, companies will draw from a pool of familiar faces that they have worked with in one guise or another over a long time.

The Deloitte Insight report (2018) codifies the change in employment practices along a continuum that starts with full- or part-time employees. It extends to joint ventures, contractors, freelancers, gig workers and even into crowd-sourced information or activity. The workplace is becoming more complex and the boundaries of organizations are becoming more permeable, and learning and focused activity on outputs is what joins these groups together and keeps them focused.

Sixteen key elements of a learning culture

Bersin leaves his webinar talking not about the technological imperative but the critical role of a learning culture in the successful implementation of these technologies. Ultimately, success is based more about people and culture, rather than software and apps. Bersin selects core factors that include a strong CLO, great L&D measures of effectiveness, and having processes for developing talent alongside values and processes that form the bedrock of a learning culture. He lists eight key elements to which I have added some commentary, and then added a further eight factors:

- *Leadership that reinforces the need to learn.* This book has shown the critical role of senior management in promoting and living the mantra of lifelong learning. This is about finding time to encourage learning and to build a culture of sharing those insights and asking for help whenever necessary. All of the companies that I have case studied have outstanding CEOs who genuinely make a difference and live and breathe learning.

- *Mentoring and coaching time from experts and leaders.* This extends from a culture of encouraging staff to ask for help, to one where experts and leaders embed their role as mentors, coaches and sharers of business knowledge into their daily leadership behaviours. They always set the benchmarks for leadership practice and define how leaders throughout the organization behave so what they do is noticed and is imitated.

- *Sharing information openly.* This is at the heart of any learning organization. Personal knowledge and expertise is important but generally increasing the collective knowledge of the whole organization is ultimately the critical difference. This is partly a learned behaviour, and partly having the right environment to look for and share answers across time and geography.

- *People are empowered to point out errors.* This point embraces the idea of failure. If no one admits failure or when lessons should be learned, then nothing is learned and the organization does not move forward. And if there is a blame culture, where displacing responsibility for things going wrong is a critical survival skill, then progress will be limited. The CEO of the WD-40 Company's mantra of 'what did you learn today?' encourages the sharing of mistakes or failed experiments and focuses on sharing the lessons across the whole company.

- *Listening to customers.* I would dramatically extend this behaviour to actively listening to customers, colleagues, as well as competitors. Active listening is a skill that needs to be acquired in a turbulent business environment. It is less common than you think, as reward is usually given to the person who speaks rather than the one who listens. Active listening means actually hearing what someone says rather than interpreting what someone says so it confirms your own view.

- *Built-in time to reflect.* We know from neuroscience that learning requires time for the brain to process. The brain needs to absorb new knowledge or expected behaviours, and complexity needs clear thought and time to work out actions and strategies going forward. Allowing an individual time to reflect is a fundamental part of this. Therefore, building reflection into day-to-day work is a non-negotiable element of a learning culture.

- *People move around and take risks.* If we relabel risk as experimentation, it is possible to innovate in even highly regulated organizations. ING Bank, for example, are trying to alter the mindset of their staff and leaders by asking them to think more like a technology company than like a bank. The result is that speed of innovation and implementation has dramatically increased. It is hard to build a learning culture in a completely risk-averse environment. Part of a learning culture is the free sharing of ideas and continuous open questioning of the status quo.

- *Experts are rewarded and valued.* I would add that experts require nurture and continuous development, as well a culture of sharing their expertise. Communities of practice help congregate expertise across an organization, and share understanding of what is best practice. They have to be free to operate and free to develop a status in the organization. Using an open network of leaky rather than closed expert groups offers sources of knowledge, and pathways to broader development. A learning culture tends to expose the 'go to staff' and put them in a more formal structure with more formal recognition of what they can contribute.

To Bersin's eight attributes I would add a further eight:

- *Staff are encouraged to take charge of their own learning destiny.* In other words, are they given the opportunity to set their own personal learning goals in parallel to the goals set by the team or the organization? Personal development should be part of staff aspiration and stretch assignments should be offered as a matter of course to reinforce the need for continuous learning.

- *There is widespread networking inside the organization, and significant connections with outside organizations and experts.* Many organizations frown on employee activity outside the company, and restrict access to conferences, forums and networks on the grounds that they distract the individual and adversely affect performance. A learning organization does the exact opposite and sets a goal for everyone to bring new knowledge into the organization on a regular basis and ensure that it is shared and embedded.

- *The focus for appraisal and review is on potential rather than only on target hitting.* Only measuring staff performance on what they did last month or last year does not measure their potential contribution to the company in the future. Failed experiments and deep learning in one period can be turned into productivity for the future. Constant success is often based on risk aversion, and covering up mistakes and short-term aspirations. More open debate and deep learning experiences build rather than destroy potential and require a longer-term focus. Visiting Silicon Valley for the first time in the 1980s, I was staggered by the openness with which people shared their failures (some of which were catastrophic) in just general discussion. I was also surprised by HR leaders telling me that they would only hire people who had failed already. Better to have failed and learned elsewhere than have someone fail on their patch!

- *The learning operation has shifted to a facilitation and consultative role rather than a controlling one.* A learning culture cannot be controlled and delivered by even the most competent learning operation. The learning organization should set the parameters and standards, create the right environment, provide useful tools, and then get out of the way and let the business and the individuals take charge. Those learning operations that seek to encourage, advise and experiment, rather than deliver and control, are the building blocks for a learning culture.

- *There is an online learning space for asking questions and knowledge sharing.* There has to be a location where staff can congregate and ask questions and get to know their peers and who has expertise in what. In Pixar Steve Jobs insisted that the physical environment included a central hub for all staff to meet informally, eat, drink coffee and generally get to know each other when the company moved to its new campus in Emeryville California in 2000 (Rao and Sutton, 2016). Cross-functional teams were also one of the features of Pixar's way of working and an important element of its success, according to Ed Catmull, the organization's CEO. In essence, challenging, answering questions, or simply joining in the discussion, is fundamental to a learning organization and a strong learning culture. In practice those spaces can be physical locations (as in Pixar's case) or online. The exact same principles apply.

- *Anyone can ask questions and expect reasonable answers.* At the heart of innovation is curiosity. Curious people (rather like young children) should be encouraged to ask why? And then why that answer? If good questions are seen as powerful learning tools, and agents for sharing knowledge, personal growth and organizational development are almost guaranteed.

- *There is a culture of open discussion of performance and customer satisfaction.* A cold hard look at how an organization performs in terms of metrics, or net promoter score, is a key element of learning. Jeff Bezos at Amazon, for example, spends regular time on the phone talking to dissatisfied customers where Amazon has got a lot wrong. Bezos wants to understand the worst that Amazon can inflict on its customers, and by understanding what went wrong, put it right structurally so it does not happen again. If you never confront how staff feel, or what the nature of the customer experience is, it is much harder to develop the impetus for innovation. This encourages learning that will generate solutions and make it right (see for examplehttps://neilpatel.com/blog/lessons-from-jeff-bezos).

- *There is widespread trust between all staff and their leaders.* I have written extensively on the importance of trust as a defining goal and it is a non-negotiable fundamental of a learning culture. With no trust, there is no honesty and openness. With no open discussion, learning is severely limited or jealously guarded and insight is rarely shared.

How do you implement technology effectively?

Donald Taylor's 2017 book, *Learning Technologies in the Workplace*, gives a practical exposition and account of the impact learning technologies have made, and will continue to make, on workplace learning. It takes a wide, sweeping perspective tracing the increasing impact of learning technologies over time, and offering a simple model for their implementation, which he calls a process model for implementation. It comprises six stages. The journey runs from understand, to plan, and then from there to test, implement and assess and finally sustain.

Figure 8.1   The six-step model

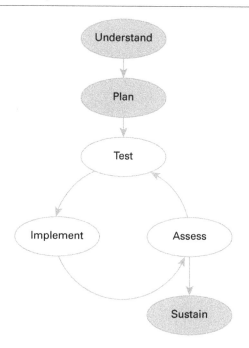

My view of this model is slightly different to Don Taylor's as my experience indicates that the process is a little more iterative and less linear, particularly in the early stages, than the illustration given above (Taylor, 2017: 87).

In my view, there is much to be gained from iterating around what the business understands it needs, and altering the implementation in the light of this understanding, as well as in the light of testing. That overall conclusions about what the business wants should be the direct driver of impact measurement and sustainability. Needs and environments can change over time, or clarity can emerge slowly. Therefore, the 'understanding' element of the model should be under continuous review as more data is accessed or external factors alter to drive change in the internal political landscape.

Don Taylor's first stage, Understand, is very important but is often omitted, even by thoughtful learning practitioners (Taylor, 2017: 90). So instead of a wild rush to implementation, it is imperative to

Figure 8.2   Reviewing understanding

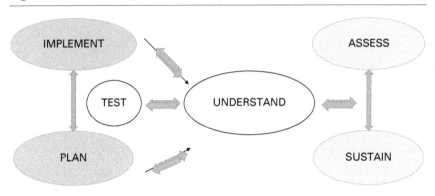

think about the approach and be clear as to what business issues are, and what problem you are trying to solve. This should include shaking out any internal political issues that are embedded and obscure. This is an important stage that should precede the sorting out of any necessary technical issues.

To illustrate this, in the early days (2002) of running the L&D operation at the BBC, I scoped out a massive increase in our use of learning technologies. This included a complete revision of our entire suite of e-learning modules to make them more interactive, interesting and far less text-based, as well as the establishment of an intranet-based site to share insights and good practice using video interviews collected on the recently available small DVI cameras that had appeared on the market and had transformed the cost and speed of video capture. This process also involved redesigning the learning site on the BBC intranet, in order to offer more immediate access to expertise, and to help staff record their learning and structure their personal development.

This was all necessary and emerged out of long discussions with potential users and senior staff around the divisions. It was designed to be an integral part of the huge change programme that was being rolled out across the BBC to deliver on the mission: 'to be the most creative organization in the world', alongside a new set of values. It was fully budgeted.

The problem was that the BBC network could only handle text, and on top of that, there was severe choking of bandwidth as soon as you tried to serve content to the smaller and more remote BBC offices. The BBC had a comprehensive video distribution network called 'Reith', which allowed programmes to be viewed across the whole of the BBC on a network of connected TVs, but it was not digital and could not be used for any other purpose. The IT operation, as huge as it was, had only distant plans for upgrading the network, as it was felt to be a low priority for the organization, compared with the urgent digitization of all production that was beginning to rear its head. The absence of a capable network, however, scuppered all our plans for a massive upscaling of our learning technology capability.

The issue was clearly not technical or technological. The upgrade path was clear. The problem was political, and an issue of prioritization. A small chunk of the huge IT budget needed to be redirected towards a significant network upgrade. The solution was not to bemoan the lot of L&D, but to set out on a campaign to explain how critical this enhanced network would be to the organization as a whole, not just our relatively small part of it. The deciding factor was when the CEO realized that his video-taped monthly briefings could be made instantly available, and downloadable, everywhere across the BBC. And that all the extensive resources developed for the 'Making It Happen' change programme could be offered to all staff to use locally as soon as they were completed rather than packaged and posted. At the time all video material was transferred to VHS tapes and posted out across the BBC.

The upgrade was commissioned, and the moment of truth came when a new highly interactive programme to explain and clarify the new editorial guidelines aimed at 1,500 journalists and 500 core programme makers was launched. We all watched nervously as thousands of simultaneous accesses of the programme began to hit the network. The group watching this were not just from L&D but a combination of staff from the IT operation as well. They too had a huge stake in its success. In the event the network survived that enormous bandwidth demand and emerged with flying colours, and it was only right that the IT staff took full credit. They had done an excellent and cost-effective job. But this small step in IT terms was L&D's leap forward technologically. That new, enhanced network was the platform on which all our technological innovation was built. It allowed rapid progress and transformation, knowing that the network could handle whatever was thrown at it. It was then enhanced as a matter of course. This allowed the network to keep up with the ever-increasing demands made on it.

The second of Don Taylor's stages is to plan the implementation, and he reminds us that this is both about the technical implementation as well as the communications plan to run alongside this (Taylor, 2017: 92). When the BBC ran its editorial policy online programme, this was the Corporation's first ever compulsory piece of e-learning, and there was widespread scepticism about whether anyone would get to the end of it, or even bother to access it in the first place! It was damned as tedious and unacceptable before anyone had even seen what was on offer. There were two core but separate exercises that went into the planning process. The first was to put the Editorial Policy team in full charge. Our people made it work well; their role was to select appropriate content that offered vivid examples of what has gone wrong in the past. Our role was to turn this into learning.

The aim was to design something that had, if at all possible, the appeal of a dramatic narrative. The idea was to grip the learner as quickly as possible by making them want to know what happened next and then alarm them with the examples of what happened when broadcast material was non-compliant, whether wilfully or through ignorance. The result was that each section was designed as a drama, and challenged the learner the minute that they began to access the programme.

The first activity was chosen carefully to make a dramatic point and get the learner hooked! We used the words of the Head of Continuing Drama (ie soap operas) to great effect when he told an assembled group that if you wanted to hook your audience you always had to begin with something dramatic that would grab their attention.

The first section of our Editorial Policy programme was set on the eve of the Iraq war. It placed the learner in the position of editor of *Any Questions?* a long-running radio show where a studio audience puts topical questions to a panel of four, made up from political, business, artistic or other walks of life. The individuals are well known, and the panel is chosen to express a wide variety of views and the aim is to achieve balance and challenge. The idea is to generate heated discussion as well as strong debate and hear a variety of opinions.

The learner in this instance took on the role of programme editor and was asked to select the four guests for that edition of the programme from a short list of 16. In doing this, politics (party representation), gender distribution and mix of pro- and anti-war opinion had to be taken into account. And to complicate the selection, the BBC had been briefed that the war was imminent, but the audience was not aware of that fact. The learner was put under severe time pressure to complete the panel. Once the choices were made, the learner got feedback on the appropriateness of the choices made and was given hints on what considerations had to be taken into account and was instructed to try again.

As this was going on, the learner was forced to deal with 'emails' coming in that demanded instant action. The most notable was from No 10, asking that the Labour selection be replaced with a more appropriately pro-war spokesperson. The learner had to decide in a few seconds whether to accede to the request, ignore it, or challenge it. Each of those three options had huge consequences.

After a final choice had been made, a full commentary was offered by the real editor of *Any Questions?* pointing out the choices she had made for that very programme and the editorial guidelines that had informed her decisions. A real challenge; and editorial guidelines set in a context that illustrated, in a few minutes, why those guidelines existed and how they were relevant and aided the decision-making process. The guidelines were crucial in that sensitive environment, and the decision to open the programme with such a case study, in such a dramatic way, was instrumental in building learner engagement.

Taylor's third stage, testing, was equally important in the development of the Editorial Policy online programme. A user group was extensively involved in testing out every element of the software, from usability, experience and content perspectives. Nothing was left to chance. And the interface that was designed became the de facto standard for all other programmes as they were developed. Everything was constantly improved at each stage of iteration and was designed in such a way that changes were as straightforward as possible. For example, the text and audio/video files were stored separately from the main coded content, so that any changes in content required did not involve extensive re-coding. This would have been slow and expensive. If the Editorial Policy team wanted a word changed at a late stage of production, it could be done quickly and without difficulty.

The Editorial Policy team owned the content, and it had to pass all their tests. But the two groups worked as a team. In all the discussions that took place between the L&D development team and the Editorial Policy experts, the only serious disagreement was over whether a user would be allowed to 'dip in' and start anywhere they chose to, in the programme. The learning team wanted to put the learner in control; the editorial team wanted the learner to follow a prescribed and logical pathway. The compromise that was finally agreed was to prescribe the first pass of the programme, and thereafter make it entirely open in terms of what was accessible when. The point about empowering the learner was possibly correct in terms of effective learning outcome, but the need to acknowledge the partnership, and the power of the Editorial Policy team was of higher priority.

Following testing is implementation. A lot of discussion was held on the merits of a soft launch versus a hard launch. The decision was between rolling it out division by division or even section by section, as opposed to a big bang launch. The decision was to make an impact and set a deadline for completion. Therefore the programme had to be launched across the whole organization at once.

Completion was not based on individuals finishing the programme, but on those individuals having a discussion with their team and agreeing what were the critical editorial policy elements that had the most direct impact on their work. This report had to be submitted by a certain deadline and acted as an acknowledgment that the task had been satisfactorily completed. A running tally of percentage completions was therefore maintained and reviewed daily as the time allocation window closed. The laggard groups were contacted individually, first by the Editorial Policy team, and finally by the Editor-in-Chief of the BBC. His email was carefully drafted and explained that he had made time in his calendar to complete the programme and had gained a number of critical insights as a result. The programme, he argued, was positively helpful. The punchline was that if he was able to make the time for this programme, no one else had any excuse for not participating. (This was all internal to the BBC. The words are designed to capture the spirit of the exercise rather than offer an attributable quotation.)

When the number of incompletes was down to a handful, direct phone calls were made. The result was that, for the first time in BBC history, the Corporation knew that all relevant staff had gone through the new guidelines and discussed the outcomes in their teams. This was a significant achievement, and did much to placate the BBC Governors, whose criticism about some sloppy programme making, and occasional poor journalism standards, had led to the initiative in the first place.

The issue of the new editorial guidelines had presented an opportunity to encourage staff to do more than remove the document from an internal envelope and place in a desk drawer. The prospect of the guidelines informing journalistic decisions and programme making before any decisions had been taken was a significant step forward. The old model of only consulting the guidelines after an editorial issue had arisen, by which time it was more than likely to be too late, was finally consigned to history.

The next stage of the model is the assessment of impact. The word is chosen carefully. Impact assessment has little to do with whether the participants liked the programme or enjoyed working through it but is more about sustainable changes in behaviour and fewer significant editorial issues arising. Editorial issues can be complex, and a document cannot – in itself – eradicate them but the discussion at team level or key guidelines and the production of local contextualization ensured broader dissemination, and since the guidelines were issued, no significant journalistic or programme-making errors have occurred. The avoidance of legal action against the BBC would have saved the BBC more than the entire programme cost. Avoiding the loss of reputation was even more valuable for the Corporation.

Something of that size and complexity could not have been delivered in a more conventional classroom setting, as the number of participants was too high, and the timescale too pressing to deliver it any other way. The fact that this limitation was turned into a triumph and moved the whole organization from a strong anti e-learning stance to, at worst, a neutral position, opened to door to other significant learning programmes built using the same technique and philosophy.

This is the subject of the final element of the model: sustain. This final phase Don Taylor describes as 'too often unloved and neglected' (Taylor, 2017: 98) as the excitement has passed and new projects are pushing for space. This is about the efficiency of implementation, continuous improvement and learning the lessons from the entire process from start to finish.

This took on a more generic resonance in the L&D team. How could we improve processes and build a better relationship with the subject matter expert, and drive forward faster? We turned this first implementation into something of huge significance that pointed the way forward for the entire learning operation. 'What could we have done better?' was a mantra for discussions between the L&D team and the rest of the organization. The responses were about speed linked to quality, and improving the network of relationships that had been set up to make the whole thing work.

Conclusions: working out what is needed and making progress

There is no escaping technology in learning, any more than it is possible to escape technology in the workplace. In order to create a realistic framework for implementation, there are a number of critical considerations, as well as some fundamental questions you should answer if you want to move forward.

1 Experimentation is vital. The habit of testing each element before committing to an organization-wide rollout is a core skill and an essential habit. What may work in theory needs to work in your context. That process of discovery builds internal partnerships and allows a coalition of supporters to coalesce outside the learning organization. Observing what happens in practice is part of the alignment with the business and a rich insight into the organizational culture.

2 Partnership is essential. The information technology infrastructure in your organization may well limit your choices. You could be pointed towards a technology that you feel is less than

optimum; however, it is usually better to work within constraints and in partnership than it is to battle against the entire organization to get exactly what you want. This is usually a futile endeavour!

3 A less than optimum technology that works well in your context is often more effective than an optimal technology that no one knows, and no one will support. There is good evidence that people will engage better with what they are familiar with rather than having to take on board something entirely new (this was one of the conclusions from the EFMD Digital Age Learning, Special Interest Group. Uptake by staff of new and existing technologies was trialled and the evidence was firmly that existing technologies made greater impact). Ease of access, familiarity, and no learning curve for use score highly, and often rate above additional functionality.

4 Ignore the adage, if you build it, they will come. Often this is naïve. You have to make a case, build a coalition of the converted and promote it like crazy. There is much evidence of new technologies sitting largely unused. The fact that they exist is no guarantee that they will be embraced. There is a lot of data now on how to make things 'go viral' inside an organization or outside (Berger, 2013). The same logic applies to learning technologies.

5 Start small and scale. Even after you have trialled and made a decision about what will work best, full-scale roll-out is probably not the best next step. A small controlled roll-out will help iron out any issues and build a firm group of supporters around the next stage of the development. It you cannot find a suitable 'unit' outside the learning organization you can use your own staff as guinea pigs and test the technology as potential users rather than providers. Companies such as Degreed (see Chapter 4) use all their staff as users of their own software in order to test out their own product first hand. Steve Ballmer, former CEO of Microsoft, and many staff referred to this as 'eating our own dog food'.

6 First ask, what is the problem this technology is trying to solve? Go back to first principles, and make sure that you have a very well-prepared answer to that question. It helps you develop your digital strategy and will give you a ready response if the investment is challenged elsewhere in the organization. Always bear the bigger picture in mind and do not get obsessed with the technology, beyond the difference it will make.

7 Grab as much information as possible before committing. Your network will always be able to help you with useful experience, or wise counsel. Share your thoughts and ideas readily. Just the process of having to explain what you are trying to do, to people unfamiliar with your organization, helps you clarify your strategy and build strong arguments for proceeding. There should be organizations you can talk to who can share experiences. Go beyond the sales pitch.

8 Start with the problem you are trying to solve and the question you want to answer, not with a technology you wish to implement.

9 See the technology in action somewhere else; do not believe the vendor when you are told that it is easy to install and will work seamlessly. Seeing it work is a significant reassurance. Talking to users is reassuring.

10 Prioritize. What do you need most urgently and what can wait a while? Do not get hooked on something that is going to be very hard to deliver, and not really a priority as far as the organization and the business benefit is concerned.

11 There are a series of questions that you should ask yourself:

- What will we be able to do that we can't do now?
- Can that benefit be quantified?
- How important is this shift?
- Are people ready for this change?
- Is the outcome proportionate to the effort required to deliver it?
- What additional (process) benefits will emerge from this implementation?
- Have all the technical issues been resolved prior to purchase?
- Have you convinced people beyond the learning team that this is a wise investment?
- Have potential users been consulted? Are they on board?

- Have you allocated responsibility for project managing the roll-out?
- Does a project plan exist?
- Is there buy-in across the organization?
- What is the plan if this whole endeavour fails?

Good luck!

References

Berger, J (2013) *Contagious: Why things catch on*, Simon and Schuster

Bersin, J (2017) Watch out corporate learning: here comes disruption, *Forbes Magazine*, 28 March 2017, accessed at: www.forbes.com/sites/joshbersin/2017/03/28/watch-out-corporate-learning-here-comes-disruption/#3e717c2edc59 in January 2017

Brooks, R (2017) Intelligent machines: the seven deadly sins of AI predictions, *MIT Technology Review*, 6 October 2017, p 62, accessed at: www.technologyreview.com/s/609048/the-seven-deadly-sins-of-ai-predictions/

Brynjolfsson, E and McAfee, A, (2014) *The Second Machine Age*, WW Norton & Company

Contrera, J and Gibson, C (2016) *Generation Z: What it's like to grow up in the age of likes, LOLs, and longing*, Diversion Books

Deloitte Insights (2018) The rise of the social enterprise Deloitte Human Capital Report, p 27

The Economist (2015) Planet of the phones, 28 February 2015

The Economist (2017) The battle in AI, 9 December 2017

Frey, C B and Osborne, M A (2013) The Future of employment: how susceptible are jobs to computerization? Oxford Martin School, University of Oxford, 17 September 2013. Available at: www.oxfordmartin.ox.ac.uk/downloads/academic/The_Future_of_Employment.pdf

Lorica, B5 AI trends to watch in 2018, O'Reilly Media Blog January 9th 2018. Available at: https://www.oreilly.com/ideas/5-ai-trends-to-watch-in-2018

Palmer, J (2017) The evolution of educational technology, LinkedIn post of 20 May 2017

Rao, H and Sutton, R (2016) Staying one step ahead at Pixar: an interview with Ed Catmull, *McKinsey Quarterly*

Taylor, DHJ (2017) *Learning Technologies in the Workplace*, Kogan Page, London

What are the essential components of a learning culture?

This book is about learning organizations and learning culture. It investigates and explores what a learning culture looks and feels like. The expression 'learning culture' is thrown around a bit too glibly sometimes, so I have tried to pin it down. Talking to individuals, exploring companies and reading widely led me to define a learning culture in terms of four fundamental components, as I described in Chapter 1. Each one has to be present if that culture is to really work for the individual and for the organization.

The perhaps surprising conclusion is that the components of a learning culture are less to do with learning and more to do with building the conditions in which learning can flourish. More learning is not the primary input. More learning occurs, in any organization, when people feel empowered. In the same way, sharing tacit knowledge is not a function of technology but rather a product of a deeply embedded culture of collaboration. Get the organization right, and learning follows. The opposite is not necessarily the case.

The four conditions are all significant, but the conversations I had with academics and CEOs led me to list trust as the most critical of the four. In a complex, often highly dispersed, working environment, where your colleagues could be based on the other side of the world, or where the people around you are all employed on different contracts and could be contract or temporary staff, or members of the 'gig economy', trust is what binds people. (For a discussion of the gig economy, see Taylor, 2017.) Trust is the basis for a common purpose and mutual support. It is the glue that holds a learning organization together.

If you work in a low-trust environment where people are deeply suspicious of each other, and survival is an intensely political game, high productivity and a culture of learning are unlikely unless driven by individual agendas rather than a collective one. A low-trust organization does not imply that there are no experts, or smart people, or unique processes that together make up the intellectual capital of an organization. What it does mean is that all mistakes are deflected onto others, blame is stronger than praise, and there is a price to pay for sticking your neck out. Good things can happen, but more by chance than design, and expert assumptions are rarely challenged and leadership is top down. People do what they are told and are not encouraged to look any further.

Low trust leads to covering up. This is as much from self-protection as it is from fundamental dishonesty. In this environment there is little experimentation, and insights are rarely shared. Julian Stodd's work (see Chapter 4) on trust in organizations has revealed, through interview and questionnaire, just how little trust seems to exist and the corrosive nature of low trust. When staff feel that no one 'has your back' and survival is keeping a low profile or deflecting blame when things go wrong, people are encouraged to shout out loud and claim victory when things go right. This is how a toxic environment erupts.

The second is collaboration. It is closely aligned, as Rod Willis showed (see Chapter 4). When there is a framework for collaboration, diversity flourishes and is welcomed. Most activities are undertaken on a collective basis, and the culture that ensues means openness prevails so that most people know most of what is going on. Openness and transparency help ensure that any insight or knowledge is shared as quickly as possible around the organization. A collaborative environment has a large number of benefits that are by-products of this process. An open, sharing workplace is usually a happier and more productive one.

Informal, as well as formal groups, gather to problem-solve. The contribution of everyone is respected, and diverse views are sought in order to gain insight. This kind of collaboration is the bedrock for innovation, along with a strong sense that 'we can do this better'. In a collaborative organization, staff enjoy work and look forward to the challenges of the day ahead. They ask for help and always feel supported. It leads to engagement and a strong sense of purpose.

The third component emerges from a high trust and collaborative culture but is also a driver of trust and collaboration. That is having a clear sense of purpose. Everyone knows what they are doing and why they are doing it. This is linked to clear values that define the organization and generate the guidelines that all staff, of whatever hue, are expected to live by.

In organizations with a strong learning culture, everyone is very clear about their own contribution and also what kind of contribution their organization is making. Staff want to work in a place that genuinely cares for customers and has a social conscience as well as goals that benefit the wider society. The best ideas and the biggest successes came from collective work, not individual accomplishment, and 'we' is far more prevalent than 'I'.

In these kinds of organizations the values are lived. Staff know what is expected of them and how they should behave. They are non-negotiable. In the WD-40 Company, the values are hierarchical, so you have to meet the first value, 'we value doing the right thing', in any challenge. Only then do the other values come into play. And the right thing is judged in terms of the company, its customers and suppliers as well as its staff. Most of the companies employ staff who fit (based on their attitude and sympathy with the mission), not just on the skills that they could bring to the table.

The final element is having formal and informal processes for sharing and facilitating collaboration. In other words, there have to be physical and/or virtual places where ideas can be worked on and problems solved. These places should be repositories of collective insight and wisdom. Sometimes the physical environment in which people work is specifically designed to enhance the opportunities to share. This is coupled with a virtual environment that encourages conversation. It is a location to seek answers as well as share ideas. The product of this is having insight permanently alive and accessible. In these cases, expertise is acknowledged and respected, and it is very clear who knows what. This is the digital equivalent of good, physical communal spaces. Both work together.

You could point out that none of these four conditions explicitly mentions learning. And that is correct. What they do is create the environment where learning can thrive. And when it thrives, it is not through more courses or programmes but as a living, constant part of the workflow. This is exactly what Harold Jarche described, when he claimed in his blog almost 10 years ago: 'work is learning and learning is work.'

The fundamental constituent of a learning culture is the overlay of constant learning on to day-to-day practice, both to inform and to guide. If each person learns something new every day, the organization as a whole improves. There is an agility and optimism at the heart of the organization and a collective sense of direction and movement. If everyone feels that they are going places, the place they work in will excel in almost everything it does. And the learning gyroscope will ensure that there is a constant view of the horizon.

Where to start and how to move forward

Taking a leaf from Carlos Ghosn: a case study of culture change at Nissan

In March 1999, Renault and Nissan announced an alliance that continues to this day. Renault invested over $5 billion US for a 36 per cent stake in Nissan, and it was agreed that the number two at Renault, Carlos Ghosn, should take over the running of Nissan. He agreed to move to Japan to assume the role. He already had a reputation as the person who had turned round Renault, but this was a much more challenging task (INSEAD, 2003).

Nissan was losing money at significant levels and had done for a number of years. Models were outdated, its market share was declining year on year, and it was over-producing cars that no one wanted. It had too many factories, with too many suppliers, and too many dealers fighting over a declining number of customers. Most sales were heavily discounted to make the cars attractive enough to buy.

The stance that Ghosn took was not to come in to tell Nissan what to do, but to change the culture of the company in such a way that it could, essentially, heal itself. Ghosn was extremely sensitive to the cultural nuances, and the negative perception of someone from outside Japan coming into such a prestigious company and telling it what to do. He was demanding, challenging, but massively empowering for those staff who he considered to be part of a critical component of senior leaders who were needed to take the company forward. He argued in a later Sanford Graduate School of Business interview that:

> When you want to turn around a company, you want to make sure that the solution is coming from inside. Anything that looks like an outside-based solution. [or] something fabricated by people coming out[side] the body of the company [will not achieve buy-in]. Maybe it's much smarter, or much more adequate, but at the end of the day, everything is all about execution, and when it comes to execution, you want people buying in, and will never buy in as much as when it is our plan... The solution is always inside. (Interview with Carlos Ghosn by Stanford University Graduate School of Business, Top Speaker Series: Irnatural, www.youtube.com/watch?v=r2gZ_23z92o)

Ghosn took three key lieutenants with him to Japan and appointed a further 12 four months later. Their job was to coach and work alongside Japanese managers to help them to a new way of working. Once achieved they could then return to France. The essence of the process undertaken by Ghosn was to treat Nissan with respect and listen to staff, suppliers, dealers and customers. From those insights, he built a vision and high-level strategy, which encapsulated the way forward.

The immediate next stage after that was to establish nine cross-functional teams that had the task of driving the company forward, and to work out the execution process for each element of the company that needed to be changed.

Each of these cross-functional teams had a specific focus, such as business development, purchasing, manufacturing and logistics, research and development, sales and marketing, finance and cost, and organization development. And each had very challenging targets that focused on the specific 'how' to deliver the change plan. For example, the business development cross-functional team's focus was to deliver profitable growth, with a specific target of delivering a plan to launch 22 new models by 2002. The purchasing cross-functional team had to show how the company could cut the number of suppliers by half and reduce costs by 20 per cent in two years.

These nine teams encapsulated the challenge facing Nissan, and the outputs were owned by the company and ultimately delivered by the company. Each cross-functional team was led by one of the French managers Ghosn had brought in, but the vast majority of their membership was Nissan staff. They worked out how to deliver the targets. Ghosn deliberately let those teams work out their own plans, without interfering. When the overall plan was launched, it was the Japanese chairman Hanawa who endorsed it. He agreed that: 'the plan is tough, perhaps even severe, but then our situation is severe. We will implement it with indomitable resolve' (INSEAD, 2003: 10).

Ghosn's focus was on learning and reframing the problems in Nissan. He coupled this with building a grand purpose and a new belief by employees that the company could achieve this turnaround in the timescale allocated. And these targets were all delivered by empowered leaders working from within. Those with the right attitude and ability were given their head. Learning was everywhere. Ghosn insisted that all executive meetings were in English so as not to disempower the French speakers (if the language was Japanese), or the Japanese speakers (if the language was French). A dictionary of 200 key terms was compiled so that there was no ambiguity about the meaning of key words. Everyone had to speak the same language, literally and metaphorically. To achieve this a large number of second language programmes were delivered.

Staff were encouraged to look outside Nissan at what other companies were doing, and bring back new ideas and perspectives. All of the standard Nissan viewpoints were challenged and changed if they were found to be wanting. You could argue that the success of the Nissan turnaround was due to Ghosn's brilliance, but a more realistic viewpoint and the one that Ghosn reiterates, is that Nissan looked deeply inside itself, picked the best people that it had to manage change and then worked out itself what had to be done and then delivered this. There was an intensive learning process that still continues and a core belief that the right people, regardless of age or seniority, should be given the space to innovate and challenge. Everyone was learning: the French managers as much as the Japanese ones.

Ten steps to build a learning culture inside a learning organization

There is no magic formula, or easy answers, but the practice of a learning culture certainly exists. This book clearly demonstrates both its existence and its power. It is potentially the foundation for survival in this complex and volatile environment.

The four components listed in Chapter 1 and reiterated above – trust, collaboration, purpose and sharing – are absolutely critical, but they do not emerge just because you want them. Here are 10 first steps that anyone can take towards building a learning culture. It may be challenging at first, but once you begin that journey it tends to move under its own momentum.

1 Look reality in the face. What is it like to work in your organization? Conduct an open and honest assessment of where you are currently in terms of trust, collaboration and sharing. Work out the most fundamental changes you have to make, then start that process. Explain the journey and get people on your side. This has to start at the top. Without that critical support you are probably wasting your time. However, confronting senior staff with the reality of what is it like to work somewhere in the middle of their organization is often enough to convince them action is necessary.

2 Define the values you wish to operate by. People will tell you want they want and what they dislike now. If you can translate that into simple values that are clear, then the entire organization can interpret what they mean for them. In other words: whatever job is being done, the values define clear behaviours. Values should always indicate appropriate behaviours at any level and for any circumstance. Any organization needs to work out what the two or three key behaviours that will encourage and sustain a learning culture are, and then begin the process of embedding the necessary change to deliver them.

3 A learning culture has to be transparent, so its implementation has to be clear and based on significant dialogue. Each team

needs to be bought in. Some space must be created for mean-ingful discussion that elaborates what this all means and takes the temperature of the organization. You cannot force a learn-ing culture on to a group of people, you can only encourage and support them to discover it for themselves. This may be tough and extended but it will help you decide the priorities that you have to focus on. Even if this is as far as you get, you will have made the organization a much better place to work and begun the process of honest and earnest debate that is fundamental for collabora-tion. This never ends; you have begun a process that you need to make habitual. Eventually, it will become the way we do things round here. However, at the beginning it may feel anything but.

4 Break down silos. Create as many cross-organizational groups as you can. Celebrate the diversity in the company and encourage staff to work across boundaries. Be explicit on how you want people to work and ensure that this is not blocked somewhere in the middle of the organization. Empower those groups.

5 Celebrate any small successes. If there are areas that you have addressed that would not have been addressed before, or ideas emerge that could not have emerged, then celebrate those changes and recognize the people who led them.

6 Encourage people to learn every day. Make space for this. Ask them to share as much of this as possible. If you make space in the work-ing day, you actually increase productivity, as staff become more efficient and effective. (See the Happy case study in Chapter 6.)

7 Create open spaces to collaborate that are both physical and virtual. (See the Pixar discussion in Chapter 8.) Physical space can be redesigned to create collaboration areas and online space can be built. The two go together.

8 Demand that all members of staff have a learning plan to develop their careers and deepen their expertise. This can be directly job related, or a way of extending a role or even shifting role. 'What did you learn?' should become a mantra that is used widely. (See the case study on the WD-40 Company in Chapter 5.)

9 Encourage people to ask questions. Ensure that there are no 'stupid' questions. Show that each person, regardless of seniority, takes the time to ask, and the time to answer.

10 Focus on challenges that the company faces. Get teams to think about threats and potential disruption in the short, medium and long term. And work on possible responses. Do not let anyone think that the job is done; this is a permanent phase. You may never succeed in building a learning culture but you will get closer and closer! It will take time, but everything should start to feel better and that consistent message should come back to you from all over the organization. This is an extended journey.

The combination of these 10 steps is immensely powerful and will engage and empower the workforce. But it will generate some challenges as well. Not everyone will enjoy a more sharing and collective culture. Not everyone sees this process as in their interests. Because it impacts on the power structure, it can be very challenging in some quarters. This cannot be ignored. Many people will embrace these changes, but it has to be clear that they are not negotiable. Anyone uncomfortable or unwilling to move has to work out whether they are going to stay or go. How long this process takes is directly dependent on how well you succeed in clarifying what is needed and how much empowerment is given to staff to work it out and build their own models and processes. If you fudge the issues, the whole process is likely to fail.

Essentially, a learning culture, like all other cultures, grows and takes shape if the conditions are right. The 10 steps are starting points to begin that process. There is no end point. The benefits of this implementation will begin very quickly, and it is up to you where you decide to stop. But at some point, there is a momentum that carries the organization forward and changes the way the company thinks about itself. Eventually you will trust the staff to take this forward on their own. Once they own the culture, they will protect it. That is not a bad place to end up.

What can we learn from Senge and Garratt?

1 Learning organizations exist and embody a learning culture. The concepts underpinning learning organization and learning culture are far from irrelevant. They represent a rich seam of investigation and exploration. However, what is equally clear, Senge and

Garratt did not provide all the answers then, and do not now. We still owe them, however, a huge debt of gratitude.

2 Garrett is too one dimensional in his analysis. His three interconnected circle model of the organization is valuable, but it does not reveal the whole picture. Senge, on the other hand, is too complex. It is almost impossible to know where to start with his five disciplines, seven disabilities and 11 laws. He offers rich insight, and his book is a worthwhile read even now, but it is also hard to leave the book without a sense of confusion and a bafflement. What do we do first and how will we know we have done it!

3 The unifying principle of Chris Argyris's double-loop learning concept (see Chapters 2 and 3) endures magnificently across time. It is a simple yet, profound means of questioning our underlying assumptions and gets at the heart of what is wrong with organizations. This understanding helps fix poorly performing companies in a way that single-loop learning, with its tendency to draw attention to the superficial causes, does not. It is as relevant now as it ever was, and its use by huge organizations such as Amazon attests to its contemporary relevance. It is simple to grasp and powerful to apply. This process powers a learning culture and emerges out of a propensity to explore and a desire to get at the root cause.

4 Returning to the thinking of the 1980s, which includes the later work of W Edwards Deming as well as Chris Argyris, reveals the common roots for the two books. Both Deming and Argyris's ideas changed the way problems and challenges were framed. It is, therefore, right to gently remind contemporary organizations of the value of these thinkers and their ideas. Modern-day manufacturing owes much to Deming's pioneering work on quality improvement, and managing complex systems owes much to Argyris's ideas. In some ways, their thinking endures with more resilience than the two books that started the debate about learning culture.

5 Attempting to understand how our complex, contemporary business environments work is profoundly relevant. Perhaps we need to revive these ideas and speak about them alongside the concept of learning culture and learning organization. They are critical tools for today.

6 The logical end point of this book is to see learning in organizations as more complex, and more powerful than many L&D departments seem to believe. We have to change that, and work with L&D to take a more holistic view.

7 The need to focus on productive learning as a way of meeting today's skill needs, and generative learning as a way of preparing for tomorrow is a very helpful way of shaping and articulating the fundamental polarity that divides the learning needs of an organization. This framework from the CRF report is extremely potent in terms of understanding one of the factors that differentiates a non-learning culture from a learning one.

8 There is still much to be discovered about the nature of learning organizations and the learning cultures that support them. New research will arise, and the concepts will receive much more attention because they help us understand and work out how to respond to uncertainty and complexity.

9 Ultimately, we see that the power of a learning culture and the means of building and sustaining it, requires much more than a souped-up learning organization. This book shows how the whole workplace and the entire leadership team need to get involved to deliver something transformative: self-healing places to work, which are productive, relevant and powerful for the people that are touched directly by them and for their community and the wider world. This is, surely, an aim worth striving for.

Ten tips for moving forwards

1 Be ambitious; building a learning culture is transformational for the learning organization and the whole company. It is therefore worth taking forward. It could be the most important task that you undertake.

2 Take your time. This is a never-ending journey and the first fruits may be slow to emerge, but if you continue in the right direction the benefits grow exponentially. If the effort seems to yield less than expected results initially, it will eventually transform the capability of the organization and ensure its long-term viability.

3 The four key components: a strong, shared mission, vision values and sense of purpose; a high-trust organization; a collaborative and innovative mindset; and a facility to share both good and bad news, are not developed linearly. You need to plan to move forward on all four and they are obviously linked. The two critical areas to push forward initially are the high-trust environment, and a clear purpose that everyone can share. These need to be kept under a watchful eye. If either slips, the whole programme slips too. There will never be a time when you no longer need to reinforce the purpose of the organization. The parameters of trust need to be tested constantly. There has to be a process that double checks the overall alignment and direction.

4 The underlying emotion that has to permeate is optimism. You have to believe in the organization and believe in the staff you have working for you, as well as those aligned around the organization. You need to believe that you can make every aspect of what you do better. This aspiration is for both customers as well as staff. As Tom Peters in his latest book *The Excellence Dividend* (Peters, 2018) claims: 'Excellent customer experience depends entirely on excellent employee experience! If you want to wow your customers, first you must wow those who wow the customers!'

5 You need to expand the amount of experimentation as a direct pathway to innovation. This needs commitment and trust to make it work. It is Tom Peters' new watchword in an acronym that may be beyond pronounceability: WTTMSASTMSUTFW! It stands for: 'Whoever tries the most stuff and screws the most stuff up the fastest, wins' (Peters, 2018).

6 Building an engaged workforce will impact on your recruitment, your induction and your career and opportunity pathways. Look at this holistically and do not pick off single aspects.

7 Ultimately, everyone will need to become a lifelong learner. The responsibility shifts to the individual; your job is to support and facilitate this, and make it happen. You cannot manage or control it. In a meta-analysis of 1,000 pieces of research on lifelong learning, the curation company Anders Pink (https://blog.anderspink.com/2018/05/what-we-learned-from-reading-1000-articles-on-lifelong-learning) summed up the conclusions from this analysis in 20 headlines. They are all relevant to this book but three are worth highlighting:

- The knowledge economy drives continuous learning.
- Change means continuous learning (and unlearning).
- Continuous learning will disrupt current learning approaches.

8 There is no way now to separate work, learning and technology. They feed off each other and each one makes demands that the other two have to respond to.

9 Tom Friedman, the *New York Times* writer and author, discussed lifelong learning in an issue of the *Deloitte Review* with Cathy Engelbert, the CEO of Deloitte US. He reflects on the inevitability of lifelong learning: 'We have to provide both the learning tools and the learning resources for lifelong learning when your job becomes work and your company becomes a platform' (Engelbert and Hagel, 2017). The changing nature of work, and the enormous consequences of technological disruption will catalyse the development of learning cultures. You can rest assured that if you move in this direction, you are moving with the flow.

10 Have fun! This should be the most enjoyable and rewarding journey of your life.

References

Engelbert, C and Hagel, J (2017) Radically open: Tom Friedman on jobs, learning, and the future of work, *Deloitte Review*, Issue 21, July 2017

INSEAD (2003) INSEAD case study 303-044-1: 'Redesigning Nissan: Carlos Ghosn Takes Charge'

Peters, T (2018) *The Excellence Dividend*, Vintage Books, New York

Taylor, M (2017) *Good Work: The Taylor review of modern working practices*, The RSA, July 2017

FURTHER READING

These are the key texts that have informed this book.

Argyris, C (1982) *Reasoning, Learning, and Action: Individual and organizational*, Jossey-Bass, San Francisco

Brynjolfsson, E and McAfee, A, (2014) *The Second Machine Age,* WW Norton & Company

Covey, S M R (2006) *The Speed of Trust: The one thing that changes everything*, Simon and Schuster

Csikszentmihalyi, M (1990) *Flow: The psychology of optimal experience*, Harper Perennial

Deming, W E (1982) *Out of the Crisis*, Preface, MIT Press

Garratt, B (1987) Learning is the core of organisational survival: action learning is the key integrating process, *Journal of Management Development,* 6 (**2**), pp 38–44

Garratt, B (2000) *The Learning Organization*, Harper Collins, London

Hofstede, G, Hofstede, GJ and Minkov, M (2010) *Cultures and Organizations: Software of the mind,* 3rd Edition, McGraw Hill Education, New York

Kofman, F (2013) *Conscious Business: How to build value through values*, Sounds True, Boulder, Colorado

Mallon, D (2010) *High-Impact Learning Culture 2010*, Bersin and Associates Research Report

McKee, A (2017) *How to be Happy at Work,* Harvard Business Review Press, Harvard

Stewart, H (2012) *The Happy Manifesto: Make your organization a great place to work – now!* Happy/Kogan Page

Paine, N (2017) *Building Leadership Development Programmes That Work*, Kogan Page

Pedlar, M (2008) *Action Learning for Managers,* Gower

Pillans, G (2017) *Learning: The foundation for agility and sustainable performance*, CRF, London

Schein, E (2016) *Organizational Culture and Leadership,* 5th edition, Wiley

Senge, P (1990) *The Fifth Discipline*, Doubleday

Stodd J (2018) *The Landscape of Trust Sketchbook and Guidebook* Sea Salt Learning, Bournemouth

Taylor, DHJ (2017) *Learning Technologies in the Workplace*, Kogan Page

INDEX

CPSIA information can be obtained
at www.ICGtesting.com
Printed in the USA
BVHW060821041119
562844BV00020B/2253/P

9 780749 482244